Become a Bestselling Christian Author

Releasing the Author Within You

Maurice Wylie

RELEASING THE AUTHOR WITHIN YOU
Copyright © 2020 by Maurice Wylie

ISBN: 978-1-8382191-4-7

All rights reserved.
No part of this publication may be reproduced, stored in a retrieval system, or transmitted in any form or by any means, electronic, mechanical, photocopying or otherwise, without prior written consent of the publisher except as provided by under United Kingdom copyright law. Short extracts may be used for review purposes with credits given.

Main translations in use:
Scripture quotations marked NKJV are taken from the New King James Version®. Copyright © 1982 by Thomas Nelson. Used by permission. All rights reserved.

Emphasis within Scripture quotations is the author's own.

Published by
Maurice Wylie Media
Your Inspirational Christian Publisher

Publishers' statement: Throughout this book the love for our God is such that whenever we refer to Him we honour with Capitals. On the other hand, when referring to the devil, we refuse to acknowledge him with any honour to the point of violating grammatical rule and withholding capitalisation.

Disclaimer
This book will teach you many things that will help towards the success of yours. For legal reasons, it does not guarantee the success of your book.

For more information visit
www.MauriceWylieMedia.com

Contents

DEDICATION		9
ACKNOWLEDGEMENTS		11
FOREWORD		13
INTRODUCTION		15

CHAPTER ONE — **Don't be scared of the dark** — 19
Giant Killer - "I have an issue with success."
Giant Killer - "I can't see what others see."
Giant Killer - "I am afraid to step forward."

CHAPTER TWO — **Learning how to possess the vision** — 24
What burns in your heart?
Directions to success

CHAPTER THREE — **Overcoming the giants** — 30
Giant Killer: "If God wants it done, He will do it"
Giant Killer: "I live by faith"
Giant Killer: "Just a hearer"
Giant Killer: "Time is my problem"
The Main Killer Giant: "I don't know where to start"
Prepping is a must!

CHAPTER FOUR — **Understanding the specifics** — 37
The role of ghostwriters
The role of editors
The role of proofreaders
The role of designers
The role of illustrators
The role of typesetters
Best book sizes
Book quality
Book cover design
ISBN
The legal aspect of publishing
Sample disclaimers
Credits
Subsidiary rights

CHAPTER FIVE	**Finding a book publisher**	**50**
	Knowing what to submit	
	Your letter	
	Be open for feedback	
	Dealing with a no offer or refusal	
	Publisher's proposal	
	Publisher's contract	
CHAPTER SIX	**So you think you've finished?**	**54**
	How to become an ambassador for yourself	
	Understanding promotions	
	Branded websites	
	Don't get caught out!	
	Good and bad reviews	
	A book trailer	
	Accounts	
	Royalties	
	SOR	
	Self-publisher's distribution and requirements	
	Show your best side with debt	
	Book transportation	
	Final stages of your book	
CHAPTER SEVEN	**It's time for a book launch**	**72**
CHAPTER EIGHT	**Time to turn up the heat**	**80**
CHAPTER NINE	**Self-publishing vs Publisher**	**87**
	Books! Books! Books!	
	Ebook or printed book?	
	Ebook or audio book?	
	What you don't want to read, but you need to…	
CHAPTER TEN	**Fast track development**	**96**
	How to create a character	
	Book stages	

CHAPTER ELEVEN	**Avoiding costly mistakes**	**100**
	Children's book with illustrations	
	Reprints	
	Writing a fiction book	
	First delivery only happens the once	
	There was only one Elvis	
	Grammar vs culture	
	Don't rob the buyer	
	Don't be deceptive with spaces	
THE LAST NOTE	**Leave an inheritance…**	**104**
AUTHOR'S PLATFORM		**106**
	Margaret Cornell, England.	
	Dr. Robert Ballard, USA.	
	Melanie O'Sullivan, Republic of Ireland.	
	Anato Swu, Nagaland, India.	
	Elizabeth Hamill, Northern Ireland.	
	Rebecca Brand, New Zealand.	
EXTRAS		**121**
NOTES		**122**

Dedication

This book is dedicated to those brave people, who even against all the odds are considering or have already taken the plunge to write their own book. As the late novelist, Toni Morrison, famously said; "If there's a book that you want to read, but it hasn't been written yet, then you must write it!"

What would this world be like without books? Imagine the void if your book was never written.

Acknowledgements

I wish to acknowledge a number of people who have helped me develop throughout my Christian walk. The two people who laid spiritual foundations into my life; my spiritual father Rev. John Hamilton, and my spiritual mentor Alexander (Alec) Schofield.

To my bestie, Mrs Maureen Wylie, my yellow rose, my everything. Thank you for all your sacrifices of time as we journey through this life together.

To our team at Maurice Wylie Media, editors, ghostwriters, spiritual overseers, proof-readers, quality control, video producers, website developers, international workers. Everyone that works crazy shifts and goes the extra mile because we want to deliver the best.

To the One and only Jesus Christ, who can take the impossible and make it possible, I am forever grateful.

To the numerous friends that hold all different positions across the world in whom I wondered who should I ask to write a Foreword. For me, on this occasion, I did not choose which one is the better known for commercial purposes. I decided to pick a man that God had laid on my heart for the Foreword. In his later years of life, God had put a message in him that he knew needed to be published. As you read his Foreword, one thing you will note… it is never about a book being published, it's about the life that published the book, after all, that was who Jesus died for – for us. Thank you, Hugh, for writing the Foreword.

Foreword

There! He has said it again. "You don't need to go there." One of the many responses to most of the questions asked about The Book of Revelation. So, I did something about it; but when was I going to publish the study that I have reviewed, twice yearly, for the past four years. It was always this time, but the old fears about grammar and editing and who knows what other unforeseen hurdles lay in wait, soon put an end to that, and fuelled the doubts of my ability to produce something worth publishing. However, as I had on many occasions, I Googled Christian book publishers in Northern Ireland and for the first time, I saw Maurice Wylie Media. They offered some of the things I needed assurance on. With my 82nd birthday behind me, time was running out: I submitted my manuscript. A face to face meeting was arranged. Maurice is the sort of person you soon think of as someone you have known for a long time; someone you could trust to tell you how it is, good or bad; so, into his hands I placed my creation.

In the Maurice Wylie crèche of improvement: what I thought was perfect, my creation, my baby, was faced by a number of probing questions, each provoking a response of deeper thought; sometimes in agreement; sometimes in defence; the outcome always beneficial, giving new insights into what I thought was complete. The whole process, a learning curve allowing you to work with a dedicated professional team; whose combined experience is at your disposal to fulfil your dream. A process of agreement by consensus, that, where required, produces text that says what you meant to say, and brings forth a book more able to face the world. A process that does not in any sense deprive you of ownership; well-rehearsed by the many that have passed through the crèche.

It is said, 'you cannot judge a book by its cover.' That may be so. However, I believe Maurice Wylie's team have shown how the cover can embrace the content of the book. I will always remember the first time I saw the front cover proposal; I was speechless for a moment at how they took what was inside me and produced a front cover picture: my immediate response was, I hope the content is as good as the cover! The balance and depth of colour used was eye-catching, giving a dynamic edge to the subject, and drawing you in to the new title of the book that from the outset Maurice asked me to consider, and which at first, I was reluctant to change. This title brought together with the picture, captured for me the essence of the content and underlined the sound judgement of Maurice and his team. On the back cover this is underscored by the way the team offered my creation to the reader. When I handled the first book and opened it, I could not have been more impressed by the text chosen by the team which was presented in a way I could only dream of; here at last expressing my long-held desire to share God's Word.

Knowing regret would come by inaction, I stood on the shoulders of Maurice Wylie Media to reach my goal. They bore the burden of my uncertainty: They exist as a conduit for God's word from the pen of others like you and me. A ministry that strives to share God's word with other Christians and witness to a sinful world.

Hugh Lindsay McKnight,
Elder, Crumlin Presbyterian Church, Northern Ireland.

Introduction

To the reader…

Most people like coming over the finishing line in what they do. Whether it's passing an examination after months of study; receiving a salary after a week of sweat at work; giving birth to a child after months of pregnancy; then feeling the sigh of relief when they cross the line. We tend to believe the finishing line is more important than the journey. But this is not so. If we understand that the journey is just as important, then if we learn from others who have gone on that journey before us, we will not have to do things the hard way. By learning from others' mistakes, we can save time and money.

I was considering writing about the mechanics of book-authoring; the how-to if you like. After all, this is what most people want - to cross the line as quickly as possible. However, the more I thought about it, the more I realised; when we learn one lesson from God, it can often affect other aspects of our lives. God doesn't just want you to write a book, He wants to change your life also as you write a book. I have purposely detailed background stories to show how God taught me, and in learning from the Master, I am now not only an author, but I can help equip other people to write and publish their books.

A truth…

The Bible tells us that *'The latter will be greater than the former.'* (Haggai 2:9) Now, the majority of us will have read this verse and never have related it to publishing a book. Yet, within it lies a key to your book success. The end of the book must be greater than its beginning. I keep this as a principle in my own life.

I don't share this out of boastfulness, but to let you see where I am now in comparison to where I was. As an entrepreneur, I run several businesses; I'm a director of several charities, serve in local church leadership, husband, father, and am seeking to see God manifested through the lives of His people. But it was not always like that. My life did not start with success, or handouts, or hand-ups; the opposite is true. But I'll let you into a little secret. If you listen to the voice of your Father in Heaven, success will follow. He will take you where your education will not, He will supply what the bank cannot; after all, the Bible says, He is our Jehovah Jireh – The Lord who provides. It's time, not just to believe, but to see God manifested through your life.

Welcome to *'Releasing the Author within You.'*

Maurice Wylie

> *Fear is only a darkness hindering you from seeing the light.*

To get the most out of this book…

May I suggest at this point that you acquire a small notebook to record some of the points which jump out at you as you read this book? At certain places in the text, there are suggestions for lists you can construct to cement or enlarge your thinking. Having a handy place to build these lists could be quite useful. When I started writing books, I jotted down ideas at the time I found them in my mind, as you will read here. There are electronic means of achieving that now, but for some, a notebook is indispensable.

CHAPTER 1
Don't be Scared of the Dark

I have never forgotten a particular day as I sat in the first-year class of high school. In truth, they had only changed the name that year from *secondary* school to *high* school: they thought the title 'secondary' belittled the students. But for me, it never bothered me what name it had: *'Just get me through another day at school,'* that was all I cared. I often thought, *'Get me to age 16 so I can get out of here!'*

That day, in English class, each of us was given a book and each pupil started to read, a page at a time. The first pupil read the first page, then the next pupil the next page and so on. Of course, here was I, counting the desks, 15 desks. I knew that I would have to read page 15.

Oh, I wish mine would have been the last desk. Better still, that there was no page count, allowing me to miss out on reading. But this day, fear and sweat started to take over my body. By the time the girl beside me had finished reading, the sweat was running down my face, my back was soaked. I opened my mouth, but nothing came out. Oh, how I wished the ground would open. I tried again and again, but nothing would come. The teacher was now insisting that I read. But nothing happened!

It was then I found out that fear and uncertainty were dominating factors in my life, rooted in childhood abuse. I felt the dark secrets beyond the years of a child which I had to carry… surely nothing good could come out of me?

Nathanael asked Philip the same question in the Bible; *"Can anything good come out of Nazareth?"* (John 1:46) Can I ask you, "Can anything good come out of you?"

Some of you will find this hard to answer; others will immediately respond, "Yes!" But, in truth, if God is in you, then the answer is ALWAYS YES! You see, if God is IN YOU, then He wants to work in you and through you. The Bible tells us in Psalm 100:5 that *'the Lord is good!'* And because He is good, only good things from heaven can come from Him; and that includes your manuscript!

A common obstacle to writing a book, whether a potential bestseller or not, is that, just like Nathanael, often we don't think outside of the box.

Every bestseller has a reason for its popularity. The book did not just fall off the shelf. Every time someone walked into the shop it wasn't crying out, "BUY ME! BUY ME! As much as we would like that, it just does not happen. Every bestseller has a reason for it being just that. What would your *'bestseller reason'* be? Write it in your notebook or below.

Think outside of the box…

I left school at the age of sixteen, with no exams passed. In truth, I reckoned I would never see past 21 years of age, because of the intense Troubles where I lived in Northern Ireland. My thinking was, *'What is the point in studying if you will never get a chance to use it? I'll likely end up dead.'*

Since I left school without qualifications, it limited my choice of jobs. But thanks are due to a kind-hearted man, who gave me a job in his start-up sawmill. I have to say; it was quite a dangerous place to work: it was before the enforcement of all the health and safety rules and regulations in businesses. (I could write a book on that.)

That year we had started to make garden sheds, and we were busy. Garden sheds were quite a new thing then, but in the winter months nothing was happening: nobody needed a shed for the winter.

I remember the first Christmas working there. Work was slack to the point that sometimes you just made noises with hammers and saws to make the boss think that a lot was happening. In truth, I knew that if we got through that Christmas, something had to change.

There's an interesting circumstance in the Bible. The Israelites had encamped at the Red Sea, feeling safe until they heard the hoofs of the Egyptian horses and chariots. At times we are waiting on God, when all the time God is waiting on us; and Moses is doing precisely that - waiting. After all the waiting and blaming God, God says to him, *"What is in your hand?"* Moses answered, "a rod". God said, "Lift it up!" (Exodus 4:2) How life would change for the better if we only realised that God wants to be God in our life more than we want Him to be.

For me, shortly after starting work, success would be to secure my job through the next winter, but how? I was not the boss; I was only the 'get-me guy!' *'Get me this, get me that.'* Then God gave me the opportunity to create.

I remember as a child playing cowboys and Indians, watching those films of how they would lock up the baddies and sometimes they would escape. And I thought, why could we not make a children's jailhouse, with an escape hatch, wooden bars on the window, etc. Without me boring you with all the details, I designed it, made it two feet off the ground, put a cell into it with an escape hatch; and that was the first time the business had work at Christmas. The following Christmas we sold more of them than we did sheds in that summer.

Why? It came out of a need; out of what was I attached to. It came out of a concept and became very successful. At that time, no-one had heard of children's houses: a totally new idea hit the market.

Two things we can learn from this. Firstly, we must hear from God; secondly, what or to whom are you connected? These are two primary keys to making something successful in your life. Oh! Did I use the word 'successful?' Christians seem to run from this word as if it had a demon attached. So, let's kill the misunderstanding of this giant.

Giant Killer: "I have an issue with success."

At school on those exam days, I would leave out some answers on the examination papers each year for the sole purpose of not moving up a level to the next class. Why? Because students in the upper-class were taught French. For me, well, English was enough.

Success has different definitions depending on who or what the person or thing is. My definition of success was 'not moving up a class.' Yet another person could look at me as having failed. Some of you potential authors could be content just having your book published, and not be concerned whether it sells or not. Some may judge that you 'failed.' But did you? Another writer could sell 10,000 copies and think they've failed because it wasn't 20,000 or 100,000. Many will be satisfied with just 100 copies printed for their immediate family. Success is relative.

Please: write down your definition of success in your notebook or below.

> *A writer will see an obstacle as a greater platform for success.*

CHAPTER 2
Learning how to Possess the Vision

Have you ever played or watched soccer? Before I ever played my first soccer match, we would have kicked ball outside my parent's home. Someone would pass me the ball, and then I would pass it to another, and so forth; in other words, we were just passing the ball, even though we called it soccer.

When I was introduced to soccer at school, I never thought more of it, other than it would be the same. I remember we had been separated into two teams on the pitch. Shortly after it started, I was close to the opposing team's goalposts. I knew the object was to shoot the ball into the net. Somebody passed the ball to me, but before I could take the shot, I was tackled by an opposing team player who won the ball and deprived me of a chance even to attempt to score.

You see, in those days our family did not have a television. All I knew about football was what someone had shown me. My definition of soccer was what happened outside my home, but the actual meaning was what happens on a pitch. My mind had to adjust to a new set of rules, to a new style. I had to learn quickly!

There is a big difference in being given something (the football) and possessing it.

God told the Israelites, "I have given you this land!" but He also told them, "Go in and possess the land." Can you now see the difference? God can give you - grant you His inheritance, but there will be giants waiting to take the ball off you, to stop you possessing it.

I want you to understand - your inheritance is never something YOU make: it is something that is given to you from a predecessor; one who has gone before you.

The Bible says, in Psalm 50:10, that *'God owns the cattle on a thousand hills.'* But can I ask, do you know anyone who has found one of these cattle? Yet, if the Bible is true, and we know God cannot lie; why have you or others not found the cattle? The answer was alluded to in chapter one of this book… Like Elisha's servant, we're not 'seeing.' If you and I were to walk into a field, we would likely see the cattle; in other words an animal, and it's likely we wouldn't notice anything else. But if a farmer goes into a field of cattle; he or she would see those cows from a farmer's perspective. They would see an opportunity to take what is in front of them and make money – they see steak, they see a harvest. They would see further than you and I did.

When the Bible speaks of the cattle on a thousand hills, it is not referring to animals that eat grass. It is referring to the fact that there are a thousand opportunities on the hills for you to prosper in God. Are you willing to climb?

The concept that God will give you will represent one of the cattle. If you can grasp that, not only will your concept touch lives and change them for the Kingdom, but it will also put money into your pocket. It could pay for your next break, a mission trip, or put your child through university. Most of all, it could fund your next exploration to find another 'hill' that has 'cattle' on it.

Your concept/vision is your main ingredient for your book. Yet, it will be opposed by your enemy, with doubts, fears etc. But we can deal with those issues and allow you to have a platform to work from.

What burns in your heart?

Some of you will need to think about this, but the question is… what is burning in your heart?

What do you enjoy talking about? When I say that, I don't mean light-hearted chat. I mean what causes joy to arise within you when you talk about it. Or how do you feel when you witness injustice? What stirs you to action? If you were to leave the world with a core message, what would it be? Now don't be going all spiritual here and saying, "God loves you!" I need you to combine those questions and write a paragraph. Let me show you how I concluded mine.

Growing up in a church in the 70s, where they preached hellfire and brimstone, the perception was that if you were not part of this denomination, you were going straight to hell. Every Sunday night, there was a different verse and a gospel message. Basically, the appeal at the end was, if you leave here tonight without being saved, you're going to hell. The preacher prolonging the plea, the music was emotional, and everyone sang sinner songs… sinners were ambushed, without realising.

Being raised in such a church, all I ever knew was their gospel message, about rescuing people from hell, even if they had to manipulate it. (Oh, did I just say that?!) My belief core was set.

I was backslidden from 12 years of age to 23. These were the darkest days of my life. When I came back to God in 1987, I was thrown back into the centre of church activity and outreach programmes, told how to dress, told to read the King James Version of the Bible, and so forth. But I will let you into a little secret: inside, I was crying. This was not the authentic me; I was being clothed like David, with Saul's heavy armour; another person's clothing (1 Samuel 17:38). We will NEVER be what we can be in God, with someone else's clothing on us.

For years I fought an internal battle, trying to be everything the local church at that point wanted me to be; but I knew I was losing the sharpness and joy of the Lord. It was then that my spiritual dad gave me a word… "Will you serve *A* church, or will you serve **His** Church?" When he said, "His Church," it was as if a fire went through my body.

It was at that moment I found the concept of my vision, calling, and purpose. I was not called to reach the lost; I was called to reach the Church. After all those years of people telling me that I was called to reach the lost, and trying to get me to go out on street evangelism etc., it was such a struggle to break free from the chains of other people's beliefs to achieve my true calling.

Now, everything I touch, even this book, to those who phone and knock on our door, guess what? Ninety-nine per cent are the Church. That is where I am free to be, and I could easily fill a book on how doors open even before I knock on them. Opportunities worldwide to make a difference happen, and when I think back… the publishing house was started for whom? For those into whom God has put a message: His Church.

When I witness that message being expressed with passion through books, joy arises within me. Righteous anger arises when religion tries to imitate the Church; it stirs me to action. If I were to leave this world with a core message, it would be… God loves His Church and seeks His Church to be all it can be upon the Earth.

What is your core? Church, youth, gardening, sport, golf, counselling, teaching, poetry? The list is endless, but God will help you focus on your core vision, purpose and calling. It will be that core of your passion that will help you achieve your results. In writing a book, if you write about something that you're passionate about, your love for it will come across. What is your core passion?

Use your notebook, or a document on your laptop or tablet, to help you remember what this book is saying to you. Put your core vision in writing.

My core is

The core then is what you have been given; it's part of your Promised Land. It is what God has caused you to dream about, chat about, have an interest in, to bring change or give insight. But God giving it to you is not the same as possessing it. Now you have to possess it, go towards it, own it. You have to take control of your destiny in God.

Directions to success…

Can I ask, 'Have you ever been lost?' Like myself, many men don't like to admit they have lost their direction. Our wife may be in the car saying, "I think we're lost." Our response, "No, it's just around the next corner!" A few corners later, you are still lost. You see; you know where you need to go – THE CORE (the location), you just need to know how to get there.

I live in a small village outside one of the best shopping towns in Northern Ireland. There are times as I am walking through the village, a car will stop and ask for directions to Belfast (our capital city). Why are they asking for advice? Because they themselves do not know the way; but they know that someone who has been there, will know.

Depending on what road they are on, I will tell them: take the next road on your right and then follow the signs. They take the next road and at the end of that road, a large sign says BELFAST and points in the direction they should go. One thing God drew my attention to many years ago was this: the closer I got to Belfast, the more signs I saw for Belfast. This is also true in what God has called you to. Once you know the CORE, look or ask someone you know who has experience for the next step. Once you take that next step, another sign will appear, then another. Before long, after you have been through all the country bendy roads, onto straighter roads and then onto the motorway, all of a sudden you appreciate the cruise control, for now, you know the destination is BELFAST, or in your case – a fulfilment of your Promised Land. The Bible says, *'signs will follow them that believe!'* (Mark 16:17) Yes, I know this does not refer to cities, etc., but all truth is parallel, and when we get to our destination, and someone asks us how we got there, our answer will be, "I followed the signs."

People who don't plan, often don't get to their assigned destination. The Bible says in Luke 14:28; *'For which of you, intending to build a tower, does not sit down first and count the cost, whether he has enough to finish it.'* Because we read the word cost, we immediately think – money. But let's open this up a little more. Cost can include not just money, it may mean stamina to finish the course, connections, know-how, plan, etc.

Sadly, many potential authors start out writing but never finish. Others finish the manuscript, and it ends up gathering dust; months, if not years, wasted. Moreover, especially if it's God-inspired; lives that could have been touched, are not reached.

> *Creativity came out of darkness.*

CHAPTER 3
Overcoming the Giants

Before we go any further, let's deal with some more Giant Killers in the Christian world and see how it affects publishing.

Giant Killer: "If God wants it done, He will do it!"

This assumption is seriously NOT true. This has been a misinformed doctrine within the Church, which has subtly stolen from the fulfilment of God's Promised Land for you.

We must level the playing field so that you know without a shadow of a doubt that it is God's will for you to enter the Promised Land He has for you. God gave the Israelites the Promised Land and told them to go in and possess it. It would never have mattered how much they would have sung and danced; how many times they would have walked around the mountain; God wanted them to possess the Promised Land. In the same way, you must decide to possess the dream He has put on the inside of you.

Take a minute and think about all the times in the Bible where God directed His people, and they then had to fight a way through something. They had to fight because there was an obstacle in their way. If we consider this saying to be true - 'if God wants it done, He will do it' - the first obstacle we encounter may cause us to walk away from the project, having been misled to thinking that God did not inspire it. This is a lie from the pit: as Ephesians 6 states, 'Having done all, stand… stand!' Or as I share in 'The Armour of a Champion'… move into a stance. We must become military combat-minded; we must take the war to the enemy. You must see it is God's will for you to complete and publish your manuscript.

Giant Killer: "I live by faith!"

When I started out as a Christian, I met some people who claimed, "I live by faith." I was in awe. I thought they lived in a superior spiritual realm which I should aspire to. Fortunately for me, I didn't. (am I allowed to write that?) God was going to teach me differently or I would have missed it.

When I meet people today who tell me, "I live by faith," I know what's coming next. "I live by faith; therefore, I have no money."

I cannot find this concept in the Bible, where one lives by faith, seeking to do something, and the resource is not there? This is not how we should define *faith*. The Bible says, *'Faith comes by hearing and hearing by the Word of God,'* Romans 10:17. Firstly, it does not say… 'hearing from a preacher on a Sunday morning.' It states, 'by the Word of God.' We know that the Word of God was Jesus (John 1), and the Bible is the Word of God. We must then conclude that faith comes from hearing from God, not man. God has deposited a *'measure of faith'* into us (Romans 12:3). In the natural, we have muscles, as it were, deposited into us. Those who exercise them more regularly have larger muscles.

The point here is that I am seeking to stay focused on why you have purchased this book.

God speaks to us and confirms it through His Word, the Bible, and in turn, the seed (measure) of faith rises to the occasion and strengthens us. Likewise, Mary, the mother of Jesus, had faith because she heard from God.

Faith, in its proper form, is a seed deposited from our heavenly Father. It began by Him, and is added to by Him each time He speaks to us. It is then fulfilled by Him through our 'possession of the land.'

Whatever God calls you to, you are in faith when you live it out. If that's a CEO, mother, husband, employee, pastor, etc., you are living in faith by doing it. Faith never relates to lack; for He who started the work (the vision) is well able to complete it with your obedience. And if we obey, we shall eat the fruit of our Promised Land.

Giant Killer: "Just a Hearer!"

How many times have we given up? Sometimes we give up easier than at other times. Sometimes we fight harder, and yet, ultimately, no matter how much we fight or pray for something, especially a loved one who's dying; the whistle of life blows and time is over. The chance we once had, no longer exists. I, for one, don't want you to live a life of regrets. As I say to leaders and Church people: When we get to heaven, God is not going to ask us how many times we attended church? He is going to ask, "Did you do what I asked of you?" You may want to get angry at this next statement, but keep reading; Jesus' primary purpose in dying for us was not so that we would go to heaven. He died for us to have a relationship with His Father. Out of having that relationship, we go to heaven. After all, would you let a stranger into your house without question? Why do we expect God to be any different?

In reading this book and in writing your book, you should have an awareness of the path that God has set aside for you; and in that awareness, you must 'take it'. James 1:22 tells us; *'Be doers of the word, and not hearers only, deceiving yourselves.'* Did you read that? If we are only churchgoers, if we are only hearing and not doing, the Bible says, we are deceiving ourselves. It's time to take off the grave-clothes and rise to the call of writing your book!

Giant Killer: "Time is my Problem!"

The number of times I have heard people say, "I know God is telling me to write a book, but I don't have the time." Can I ask, 'Did God not know you were going to be born?' Unless you believe differently, I would say that the Eternal God was able to look through time and see who was going to be born upon the earth. He allocated 24 hours in a day: how about that? The problem is not that you don't have enough time: the problem is time management. Can I ask what or who you love the most? You will find you have time for whatever that is. It could be your job, your TV soaps, or it could even be ministry; but if you don't set priorities, your time won't be efficient.

God gave Noah building instructions, but God did not turn up until he was finished; and the only way to finish satisfactorily, was to build according to God's orders.

I remember hearing a story about a young man who lived with his parents and worked a part-time job. He saw his girlfriend most nights, went to football on Saturday, church on Sunday, and was really busy. Any spare time he had, you would find him socialising with his mates, or gaming. On hearing a sermon one Sunday, it instilled in him a desire to devote more time to God in prayer. The only time he had, he thought, was one hour before going to work. So, his thinking was: come Monday morning from 7.15 a.m. - 8.15 a.m. he would pray, then wash and go to work for 9 a.m. On Monday the alarm went off at 7.15 a.m. He rolled over, switched the alarm off and went back to sleep. When he awoke, he had just enough time to get washed, and then rush off to work. But he promised himself, tomorrow morning I will do it!

The next morning, the same thing happened. He switched off the alarm, went back to sleep, then hurriedly washed and left for work. This happened four mornings in a row. On the Thursday night of that week, he attended the youth meeting. He shared with his pastor that he desired to spend more time in prayer, but it was not working, hoping for a sympathetic response. The pastor said to him; "The thing you end up doing, is the thing you deem more important at that particular time." Meaning, when he rolled over to switch the alarm off, that was really what he wanted to do; wanting to lie in more than he wanted to pray. It's the same with a lot of things; we often do what our flesh tells us, rather than what our heart tells us.

Whatever you love the most, you will put first. Create order within your life, prioritise what you want in the future. If you want a happy wife or husband in the future, prioritise time for them now. If you wish to have an anointed ministry, it comes through spending time with God now. And if you want a bestselling book; guess what? Yes, you need to spend time making it happen now.

Remember, God knew about you, therefore use the next 24 hours wisely; and continue to do so. It's not about being busy; it's about being effective. Prioritise!

The main Killer Giant: "I don't know where to start!"

When people discover I am a publisher and author, one of the most popular questions is, "I want to write a book, but where do I start?"

My answer is always the same – "Just start." Their response is "But where?" I say, "You just start" Start to write what is within you, whether it's a thought, a storyline, a chapter heading; whatever you don't have, don't worry about it.

For example, I could have the title of a book, a chapter heading, a storyline, or a thought, and have nothing else. I just start to write out what I have; that is the key. And then I keep on going to the next storyline or thought, etc. You can sort them into order later.

People will ask us how we came up with specific titles or chapter headings. It's a thought that could have come before, or, more often, during the writing. The author could say something, and it sparks something inside you. Or the theme of the book starts to unfold and, 'bang' - the title comes.

You see, the key is not to waste time on what you don't have, e.g. title, chapter headings, etc., but use the time you have, with what you have in your mind; write!

Then another thought or storyline will come, and you write it down. You may think: "but that does not flow with the other part." Don't worry about that. This is where cut-and-paste is so useful to editors. They will move that into the right slot, but editors can only move around what they have: so, write.

After a period of writing, you will see what we call a 'thread' through the storylines. That is the key to connecting them. It could be that the stories all relate to fear (or another topic), but yet you have not even used the word 'fear.' This then will lead to title suggestions. You can ask friends; "Hi, I am writing a book where the underlying theme is fear, and the storylines are: etc., etc. Do you have any idea what title I could use? Suddenly, not only will you have feedback, but that person is likely to say, "I didn't know you were writing a book?" That's what is called 'free promotion'.

At times we don't know where to start, because it's unfamiliar territory. This is where one can hand over the whole manuscript to a publisher, and they can help you write it, or they can provide ghostwriters. But let's say you want to start to write your own manuscript. Let's get set up...

PREPPING IS A MUST!

God is speaking to us all the time. We need to be aware that He speaks through our daily lives: what we see, what we hear, what we think.

On my phone I have a notepad. I use it to write down thoughts and ideas; it's my second memory. The other part I use is the camera. Where possible, I will take photos of something that I believe can be used somewhere, or perhaps just record the concept of it. Another is an audio recording device on my phone. I can immediately record an interview. Later, I can play it back and type it out. All the above is available on a smartphone.

In the past, I would have had a notepad beside my bed, and one in the car – both with a pen ready. Here is a piece of advice for you - never allow yourself to have to go and look for a pen: if you do, it may be too late. You'll likely forget what you were thinking. These days, my phone sits beside my bed. If I am awake, I can type the thought into the notepad; otherwise, if I'm exhausted and can't get my eyes opened, I press record and whisper the idea into the phone. The next day I play the recording and the thought comes alive again. Then it is transcribed.

Whether you use Microsoft Word, Google Docs, (more information on different sources are at the back of the book) or a pen, always remember to write it down. The notebook you use while reading this book might be your starting-point. If using electronic devices, remember to save your work on a digital cloud, or external drive. If your computer ever stops working, or your laptop is stolen, at least the work you have completed will still be available. Oh, the number of hours I lost when a computer stopped. Remember – SAVE, save, save to another device.

CHAPTER 4
Understanding the Specifics

The Role of Ghostwriters...

A ghostwriter is someone who you can hire to write your book, so you don't have to do it yourself. But there are keys to having a good ghostwriter.

Before we started publishing, an American minister friend sent me his manuscript and asked if I would read it and give him feedback. When he rang me a few days later, expecting to hear my enthusiasm for it, he became very deflated when I told him he did not write it himself.

He said, "How did you know?" I said, "Because it was not you." You see, how it was written, the words that were used, the style, etc., was just not him. In practical terms, it means when you read his book and then hear him preach, you would think they are two different people. God said to Gideon; "strike as one man" (Judges 6:6). That is a major key in ghostwriting.

I can tell you numerous stories relating to the outcomes of our ghostwriting team, but here's just one. I remember standing beside one of our authors one night in a meeting when this lady came over and said, "You know, as I was reading your book it felt as if you were sitting over the other side of my coffee-table sharing with me." The lady had known the author personally for over 30 years. To us, that is the highest compliment one can achieve regarding ghostwriting.

The Role of Editors...

There are numerous types of editors employed throughout the book industry, but I'd like to narrow it down to just two types: the good and the bad.

Never accept that just because someone has a title, they are good at their job. Always ask to see a sample of their work. If they pass that test, then ask them to edit a selection of your work. Remember, an editor is not a proofreader, so the comma or full stop is not their priority. For example, there have been times when our senior editor (with me or without me) has been recording interviews, or going through a manuscript, and it needed more information, or less, to give the story impact. Too many (or too few) words, not enough solid storyline. The object of a good editor is to take what you have done and maximise the content of your manuscript.

Recently, a manuscript appeared on my desk, with a request that I advise the client as to its state of readiness for publication. When I spoke with them, they were startled when I told them it needed more work. It turned out that they had already paid a Christian company £2000/$2500 for editing services. When their work was returned, it was evident that it was still sub-standard. They then hired another Christian editor who charged the same amount. Then they sent it to us for publishing. I have to say, I was as much hurt for them as they were. They had misspent thousands of pounds, and the manuscript still wasn't ready for print.

Take heed and let me repeat: "Never accept that just because someone has a title, they are good at their job." I may have just saved you thousands in that statement.

These are the most important copy-editing checks…
1. Line-by-line edits.
2. Grammar, punctuation and flow.
3. The reader's A-Z journey.
4. Voice consistency.
5. Subtle lead-generation.
6. Proofreading.
7. Scripture checks.
8. Spiritual insight.
9. Presenting your book as a funnel.

The Role of Proofreaders…

If I need to review a manuscript, I always learn something from the editor or proofreader. I find them to be smart cookies. Never be too old to learn something new!

When I was writing *A Bride Prepared for the Master*, I remember going through the finished manuscript several times and was satisfied that I had eliminated all the mistakes and was ready to publish. But let me give you very important advice here: What you don't know, you will not see.

Getting ready for typesetting, God spoke to me and said; "Did My Son not die for the scholarly as well as the less-educated?" I remember answering, "Yes He did!" Then He said it again, and I thought, "is there must be something I am missing here?"

I gave the blurb (wording on the back cover of the book) to a friend who was very academic, and asked him to read the roughly 300 words. He said, "you're using 'is' when you should be using 'are' in several places." A scholarly person will not buy the book if they observe simple mistakes." How it hit me what God had said. You see, no matter how much revelation or God-given messages you have; if it is not packaged right, not all of those who Jesus died for will receive it. In their mind, if a simple grammatical error has been overlooked - does the book have credibility?

The Role of Designers...

I have learned some hard facts regarding designers - or so-called designers. They operate on different levels. One may work in the 'self-published' style, which is normally more basic in concept. Then there's a higher level that requires more thought, more detail, and a more sophisticated, eye-catching colour-flow and design.

Just because the job title says they are a designer does not mean they are professional. You must always see a sample of their work and ask what their fee is. I need to highlight this: **Do not pay per hour.** I remember using a designer, where the design should have taken no more than one day. However, when the bill arrived, it was for a week's work, as that was how long it took them. All of a sudden, what you thought you were paying has increased, and may well exceed your budget.

You need to give the designer a concept; perhaps send them some images in the style that you are looking for. This will save time and money.

The Role of Illustrators...

People often think that the designer and the illustrator perform the same role, but they don't. The designer's focus is to take images and manipulate them to create something else. The illustrator will use a

Understanding the Specifics

freehand electronic pen to draw on a blank screen. These illustrations can range from cartoon sketches to very detailed work. Combined, they can make a high-class illustration, in colour or black-and-white. Remember, your book cover is one of the most critical parts of your book; don't try to skimp on the cover, for in the long run it will cost you - in sales.

The Role of Typesetters...

As with any of these titles, you need to see their work. A typesetter will take your manuscript, e.g. from a word document, transfer it to their software and lay out the book accordingly. You then will receive your manuscript from them, normally in a PDF format to review before print. Just because everything looks good in PDF does not mean it is ready for printing. A little nugget is, print off the PDF, making sure that the opposite pages are on the right sides. Check each page, as you flip it over, note if it relates to the other one. You can have something on one page that really needs to be on a different page. A printed manuscript will show this more than a PDF. If you don't have a printer, save your document to a USB stick, and take it to an office supplies or other outlet that provides a printing service. Often, for an extra few pounds/dollars, they will bind it, making it hugely more effective in allowing you to see any mistakes in the typesetting. Highlight any errors with a pen, and then email the reference points back to your typesetter or publisher.

Other Important Publishing Information...

Now that we have explored the roles within publishing; let's look at the mechanics of putting your book together. Here is some information with which you will need to familiarise yourself.

Best book sizes...

Book sizes are primarily determined by what country the printer is going to print in, because they can only use the paper that's accessible. We have several commercial printers across the world who allow books to be printed in higher quality than POD (Print On Demand). Some presses work off a 16-page spread, which means your book is held in 16-page blocks. Each block costs you money, so if you have a 33-page book, it is wiser to bring it back to 32 pages (2x16). This is to avoid ending up with blank or wasted pages. If you need extra pages, fill them out with promotions, or place a double-blank page at the front and back; or you might find a blank page goes well just before the start of another chapter. There are ways of handling pagination to make the book look good.

Size matters when it comes to printing. Our books are normally printed 229x152mm/9x6 inches, which is bigger than the British standard, which is 210x140mm/8.5x5.5 inches. When you are choosing a size, visit a local shop that sells books and imagine your cover being on the books and then decide what size you would pick. This is very important, especially when it comes to pricing, or children's books. Due to trim sizes, always ask your publisher or printer for advice, as they could be slicing off paper that you're paying for, while all the time you could have had a bigger-sized page. Never be afraid to ask.

Book quality...

We must remember that people have moved on from the day the tract was photocopied 100 times and one was still expected to read it, because it was Christian. Today's generation is into the latest high-tech games and high-quality graphics. We must at least match the quality, or better. There are no shortcuts to quality. It may cost more, but remember, if yours is a Christian book, then you are representing the

King of kings. Have a well-designed cover with well-written text back and front - Use 80gsm or heavier paper for the inside, and 300gsm or heavier for the cover. At MWM we will generally use a gloss cover.

Book cover design…

When people are choosing a book, the only thing that will distinguish yours from the others is the cover. Take a walk into a book store and check out the covers. Ask yourself, which one stands out for you; and then ask yourself why? Imagine your book on the shelves, in among others in the same genre, and ask yourself, 'what will make mine stand out?' If need be, purchase a couple of books that display a design that you like. Then send a sample to your designer.

Here are some things to keep in mind…

1. Colour schemes and aesthetics that appeal to your ideal audience, and which are on-brand.
2. Clear title, subtitle and author name. If a famous person writes your Foreword, also have that on the cover. Remember it's Foreword not Forward/Foreward which is a common mistake in self-publishing.
3. A well-written (and well-positioned) blurb on the back cover.
4. Author image and short bio on the back cover.
5. Book title, author name and publisher monogram (where relevant) on the spine.
6. Professional typesetting throughout.
7. Contents and index-creation where necessary.
8. ISBN for shop sales.

ISBN...

The **I**nternational **S**tandard **B**ook **N**umber (ISBN) is a numeric commercial book identifier which is intended to be unique. Publishers purchase them from an affiliate of the International ISBN Agency.

An ISBN is assigned to each separate edition and variation (except reprintings) of a publication. For example, an e-book, a paperback, and a hardcover edition of the same book will each have a different ISBN. The ISBN is ten digits long if assigned before 2007, and thirteen digits long if assigned on or after 1 January 2007. The method of assigning an ISBN is nation-specific and varies between countries, often depending on how large the publishing industry is within a country.

Here are some reasons why you should purchase an ISBN for your title…

- An ISBN improves the likelihood of your book being found and purchased.
- An ISBN links to essential information about your book.
- An ISBN enables more efficient marketing and distribution of your title.
- Most retailers require them.
- Correct use of the ISBN allows different product forms and editions of a book, printed or digital, to be differentiated clearly, ensuring that customers receive the version they require.
- An ISBN helps you collect and analyse book sales data.
- An ISBN ensures your book's information will be stored in the 'Books In Print' database. 'Books In Print' is consulted by publishers, retailers and libraries around the world when searching for title information.

Understanding the Specifics

- The ISBN conveys no legal or copyright protection, but the use of ISBNs for publications is prescribed by law in some countries.
- In some countries, a book will be charged higher tax if it does not have an ISBN.
- ISBN is the global standard for book identification.
- If you wish your book to be sold in shops, it is expected the book will carry an ISBN barcode.

You can purchase an[1] ISBN at the following…

UK/Ireland - www.nielsenisbnstore.com
(1 = £79: 10 = £164: 100 = £369: 1,000 = £949)

USA - www.myidentifiers.com
(1 = $125: 10 = $295: 100 = $575: 1,000 = $1,500)

Amazon will give you a FREE ISBN with your book. But remember, if they do so, they will then list the book as Amazon being the publisher and not you.

The legal aspect of publishing...

Some Christian authors seem to overlook the legal implications of writing for the public domain. As a publisher, we will always seek to protect our authors from legal proceedings. If an author does not take our advice, however, then they will be responsible for the outcome. For example, the risk of slander must be avoided, even if it involves a culprit whose guilt is widely known (even by the dogs on the street). If, in your writing, you assume guilt without sufficient evidence, you could find yourself in court: That's the law.

[1]*Prices are correct at time of publishing.*

Every published book has a legal page, here are some things you will find on them…

Bible quotations: For many of you, this will be difficult to accept, but the verses of any Bible translation are protected by copyright and only a certain number of verses are allowed to be used in any book, unless you receive written permission from those who published that particular Bible version.

Here is a number of the most common Bible permissions that you need to have in your book if you are using their translation:

New King James Version (NKJV)
Scripture quotations marked NKJV are taken from the New King James Version®. Copyright © 1982 by Thomas Nelson. Used by permission. All rights reserved.

King James Version (KJV)
Scripture quotations from The Authorized (King James) Version. Rights in the Authorized Version in the United Kingdom are vested in the Crown. Reproduced by permission of the Crown's patentee, Cambridge University Press.

New International Version (NIV)
THE HOLY BIBLE, NEW INTERNATIONAL VERSION®, NIV® Copyright © 1973, 1978, 1984, 2011 by Biblica, Inc.® Used by permission. All rights reserved worldwide.

English Standard Version (ESV)
The ESV® Bible (The Holy Bible, English Standard Version®). ESV® Text Edition: 2016. Copyright © 2001 by Crossway, a publishing ministry of Good News Publishers. The ESV® text has been reproduced in cooperation with and by permission of Good News Publishers. Unauthorized reproduction of this publication is prohibited. All rights reserved.

New Living Translation (NLT)
Holy Bible, New Living Translation, copyright © 1996, 2004, 2015 by Tyndale House Foundation. Used by permission of Tyndale House Publishers, Inc., Carol Stream, Illinois 60188. All rights reserved.

The Message (Message)
All Scripture quotations are taken from *THE MESSAGE*, copyright © 1993, 2002, 2018 by Eugene H. Peterson. Used by permission of NavPress. All rights reserved. Represented by Tyndale House Publishers, Inc.

New American Standard Bible (NASB)
Scripture taken from the NEW AMERICAN STANDARD BIBLE®, Copyright © 1960,1962,1963,1968,1971,1972,1973,1975,1977, 1995 by The Lockman Foundation. Used by permission.

Sample disclaimers…

(If you feel the need to place a disclaimer, then there could be a need to run the piece in question past your lawyer, for assurance that the disclaimer you are placing is sufficient.)

"Some names and identifying details have been changed to protect the privacy of individuals."

"This is a work of fiction. Names, characters, businesses, places, events, locales, and incidents are either the products of the author's imagination or used in a fictitious manner. Any resemblance to actual persons, living or dead, or actual events is purely coincidental."

"I have tried to recreate events, locales and conversations from my memories of them. In order to maintain their anonymity in some instances I have changed the names of individuals and places, I may have changed

some identifying characteristics and details such as physical properties, occupations and places of residence."

"Although the author and publisher have made every effort to ensure that the information in this book was correct at press time, the author and publisher do not assume and hereby disclaim any liability to any party for any loss, damage, or disruption caused by errors or omissions, whether such errors or omissions result from negligence, accident, or any other cause."

"This book is not intended as a substitute for the medical advice of physicians. The reader should regularly consult a physician in matters relating to his/her health and particularly with respect to any symptoms that may require diagnosis or medical attention."

"The information in this book is meant to supplement, not replace, proper (name your sport) training. Like any sport involving speed, equipment, balance and environmental factors, (this sport) poses some inherent risk. The authors and publisher advise readers to take full responsibility for their safety and know their limits. Before practising the skills described in this book, be sure that your equipment is well maintained, and do not take risks beyond your level of experience, aptitude, training, and comfort level."

Credits...

You may want to give credit to the people who contributed to the making of the book, especially if you are a self-publisher.

If credits are to be given, they are normally on the legal page; letting the reader know the people who contributed to the making of the book. Most books today do not use a colophon (information about its authorship and printing).

Here are some examples:

Cover Illustration Copyright © 2020 by (Name or Company Name)
Cover design by (Name or Company Name)
Book design and production by (Name or Company Name)
Editing by (Name or Company Name)
Chapter opening illustrations © 2020 (Name or Company Name)
Author photograph by (Name or Company Name)

Subsidiary rights…

Subsidiary rights are very common in publisher's contracts, and yet most authors don't appear to know what the term means, even after they've signed a contract.

Subsidiary rights usually are anything related to, but beyond the printed book. For example, the publisher could create an E-book for you; a t-shirt brand with your book title on it; Hollywood could make a film based on your book, and so forth. Some of you may already have signed over your subsidiary rights; I can hear your running to your contract: What did I sign away?

Within those rights some publishers will take 100%, others less. The most common is 50% to the publisher and 50% to the author.

I personally think this is an unfair split, as it is the author who put in the effort to write the story. At MWM our agreement is 75% to the author and 25% to us.

The key to ghostwriting is Judges 6:6

CHAPTER 5
Finding a Book Publisher

There are many publishers out there, but the key is to find the right one for you.

If your content is Christian, then it may be better to move towards a Christian publisher. Why do I write 'may be?' As I have said before, check them out, never be in a rush, make an informed decision. Read the small print carefully, especially regarding copyright, printing rights, subsidiary rights and whether you have the security of sign-off permission before it goes to print.

A simple way to find a publisher is to think of a book that you liked. Within that book will be the publisher details… contact them.

Visit a local bookshop and check out the books again: publisher details are in them also.

Do you know any authors? Ask them for advice!

Then, of course, if you have internet search available, you don't need to limit yourself to a local publisher. You need to find one that can take what you've written, and present it to the readers in an attractive and easily readable form. That is the key.

Knowing what to submit...

Visit publishers' websites, and you'll generally find the submission guidelines there. That's where you can confirm whether they accept unsolicited material and see what genres they accept.

Whilst every publisher has unique requirements, the most common materials you'll be asked for are; a summary of your story, an updated CV, and a query letter. (see below)

Do your research and submit exactly what is requested of each publishing house you are interested in. It's a tough market out there, so don't waste your time, or theirs, by failing to review and follow the guidelines.

If you're not the best at grammar, ask someone to check what you are sending before you send it. Bad grammar can immediately close the door for you.

Your letter...

A query letter is your first chance to get a publisher excited about your work. Your letter should not only describe what your book is about, it should explain why you're the right person to write about the subject. This is particularly so in the case of non-fiction. For the synopsis part of your letter, stick to the main highlights. No one expects you to condense hundreds of pages into a paragraph, so think about the main theme or a central event in your story.

Know your strengths and show publishers why they should invest time and money in you. For example, mentioning that you have a large social media following can also be helpful in your pitch. Perhaps you could say that you speak in front of so many people per year. As much as the publisher will be interested in who you are, they will also want to know who is around you.

Your letter is your big audition. Get it right. Check your spelling. Convince them you're the one.

Be open for feedback…

Even before you sign on the dotted line, you should be prepared to receive some feedback. Whether you pitch to an agent or publisher, both will offer you advice on how they think your first draft can be improved.

Dealing with a no offer or refusal…

One thing to remember, don't take it personally. If a publisher doesn't make you an offer, it's not the end of the world. It's just the end of that publisher for now. Every publishing house normally has an informal checklist of things they are looking for: a 'hook,' or originality; but it really comes down to whether they feel you're a good fit.

Publisher's proposal…

If your manuscript is accepted, some publishers will send you a proposal in the first instance, to ask what areas you wish to proceed with. For example, in our proposal, we will offer the publishing deal, and check to see if the author requires a branded website from which to sell their books. Perhaps also they might like to have a video trailer to promote their book; or a PR campaign, etc.

Publisher's contract…

Whether you need to reply to the proposal, or you've just received a contract, you will normally be given 14-30 days to return it signed and any monies paid. It is important that you understand the contract as you could be signing over your rights and limiting what you are able to do with your manuscript at a later date. Don't be scared of asking questions. Keep a record of the publishers answers as this would be legal evidence should anything happen.

> Never accept that just because someone has a title, they are good at their job.

CHAPTER 6
So, You Think You've Finished?

For many, this might be bad news, so please feel free to sit down before you read the next part. You've finished the manuscript as best as you can, you've revised each heading and are all set for success. Not so: this is where the real work now starts, especially if you're an up-and-coming author.

This stage is like when you have just purchased a car. You're so excited as you see it shining in the light. You've been handed the keys, (the finished book) to find out there is no fuel in the tank. You need insurance and road tax. The number of authors I have come across that think, 'the book is finished, now it's time to sit back and receive a cheque.' It's unreal! In real life, this is not how it works. Now you need to put together a marketing plan. "Oh?" I hear many of you saying, "no way! I have no experience; it's just not me." But it can be you, and I can show you how.

How to become an ambassador for yourself...

Take a pen and piece of paper and write down 20 names of people that you know, that you can have a conversation with.

Let me help you: Your parents, aunts, uncles, brother, sister, bosses, work partners, minister, elders, members of your church, or a club, hairdresser, dentist, garage, shops that you frequent, children's teachers, etc. You should be well over 20 by now, so let's list them in your notebook or below, by name first: Don't focus on the profession. Use the following headings. You are making room on the list for the professions to be added, but for now, just concentrate on the names of the people that God helps to bring to mind.

So, You Think You've Finished?

Ideally you should fill at least 20 lines with names. If you have more than 20, just keep writing. The more, the merrier. I know you can do this.

	People I know **NAME**	**Their** **PROFESSION**
1.		
2.		
3.		
4.		
5.		
6.		
7.		
8.		
9.		
10.		
11.		
12.		
13.		
14.		
15.		
16.		
17.		
18.		
19.		
20.		

Once you have them listed, write down their profession beside their name. The reason you have not done this so far is that it is important to keep focused on the connections you have.

Now, let's focus on the names that you've listed. For each one that you know, they will know someone else that they are close to, but you are not. For some, you will know one person, for others you may know several, e.g. they could play for a club, and you may have met their friends, perhaps only once. Now I want you to list below or in your notebook, the names of the friends of the people who are on your first list… This may only give you a few names, but feel free to write more.

People I know **NAME**	**Their** **PROFESSION**
1.	
2.	
3.	
4.	
5.	
6.	
7.	
8.	
9.	
10.	

So, You Think You've Finished?

If you know their profession, then add it to the list.

This is where it gets interesting. I want you to analyse the professions you have listed: for example, 'Hairdresser.'

TYPES OF PROFESSION

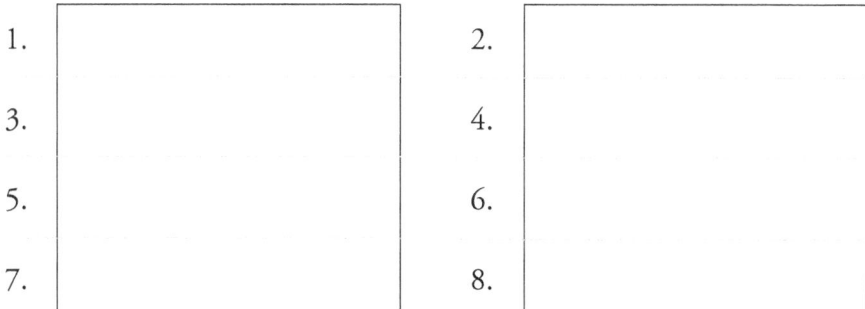

1.
2.
3.
4.
5.
6.
7.
8.

Out of those professions you have listed, you will realise that trade people will know people in the same trade or even other trades. For example, as a publisher, even though I am not a designer, printer, proofreader, etc., I know people who do those jobs. Likewise, people in the professions you've listed may know someone else you need to connect to.

Each name/profession you have listed gives you an entrance to them as someone to sell your book to.

All of a sudden, you have at least 20 potential sales. Then simply ask them if they know anyone that might be interested in your book? Remember to tell them in advance that you're publishing a book and you'll keep them a copy; it's only £10 or whatever? If you've listed 50 referrals, that's a potential return of £500.

You may wish to give immediate family members free copies in return for some social media advertising, etc.

Important...

When you speak to the people on your list, you may be amazed at who knows who. I remember one time, sharing about publishing a book to a friend. The guy said; "My friend runs a television station, I'll speak to him and get your author on." Three months later, the author was sitting in front of a television camera telling his story!

Understanding promotions...

Your object is to obtain a slice of the pie; but are you hungry for success? Or let's say it like this: are you hungry for results? We're saying the same thing, but it comes back to mindset and how we think.

In the past, promotions used flyers, posters, invites, etc. But today, we live in communities driven by social media. This is to be embraced with care. For example: do you know that there are 3.8 billion social media users in the world? In numbers it looks like 3,800,000,000 people. Imagine if you had a percentage of those buying your book. Not only will your book sales change your life, but if your book is intended to be helpful to others, look how many people you could help.

Here are some social media stats:

Facebook	2.6 Billion
YouTube	2 Billion
WhatsApp	2 Billion
WeChat	1.2 Billion
Instagram	1.2 Billion
TikTok	800 Million
QQ	694 Million

Sina Weibo	550 Million
QZone	517 Million
Reddit	430 Million
Kuaishou	400 Million
Snapchat	397 Million
Pinterest	367 Million
Twitter	326 Million

(Source: J. Clement July 24, 2020)

Now that you've started to get the word out through your list, it's time to expand even further. You can set up a page on any of the social media sites, and you can call it the title of your book, or if you're doing a series of books, then you need to name it accordingly. Then, from your own personal social media account, you can invite people to like it. Suddenly you are now building up your social media standing, and you've done it without spending money.

From these accounts, you can have an interaction with your followers. For example, you could have several book covers designed and then invite them to choose which one they like; or ask whether they would suggest any changes.

The following week you can post your cover, or title of your book, or a paragraph out of your book, etc. Then each week, you can add another post. People like personal details; most are inquisitive, even Christians: oh, did I say that? You can create a weekly diary and put in your good and bad times; this keeps them hungry for more.

Then you announce a book release date and allow people to pre-order. Now sales can start; but before that happens, we need to secure the sales.

In this day and age, social media is one thing; but when someone hears your name, or title of the book, etc., they search the internet for it. They do not look up Yellow Pages (do they still make them)? If I were to Google your name into the internet, what would come up? You should just go ahead and try it now. Type in your name and press 'search.' I remember saying that to a person one time and they did it in front of me: only to find out that another person was imitating them.

Also, if you have the title for your book, type it in and see what results come up. It may lead you to change something: even the title.

Branded websites...

At Maurice Wylie Media, we love branding, more than just building a website. Anyone can create a website. But let me explain the difference between a website and a branded website.

A website carries information, in word or picture format. Please remember, your website is a reflection of you. If it is not professional in every aspect, visitors may assume you're the type to take short-cuts. They may make a judgement on your book based on what they see on your site. A negative perception of your site may adversely affect sales. You don't need that.

A branded website, everything from wording, images, layout, colour coding, is designed to draw the visitor into your site to obtain maximum results. A little note here: if it takes more than three seconds for someone to find what they are looking for on your website, you need it revamped. Remember, websites are about speed. The homepage should draw the person in, but at the same time hook them to what they are looking for. The next click on the site should lead them to the information that they require. It's not a puzzle that you are seeking to build on a website; it's a runway to an end result.

Don't get caught out!

There are numerous web-hosting companies now throughout the world. Each one has benefits and drawbacks. With my first website many years ago, the offer was a low price per month, which enticed me as I was just happy to have a website. After 11 months they gave notice of a price increase: the price rose dramatically at the end of the 12th month period; so much so, I had to look elsewhere. However, they would not allow the site to be transferred, as it was built with their software. As a result, I had to pay for a whole new site. But this is what I learned from that experience.

Always ask before you sign up, what their renewal rate will be after 12 months. If you don't get a satisfactory answer, then ask; "How much was it last year? How much was it the year before? That information will give you a good clue to the price after 12 months, allowing you to make an informed decision.

By now, you should have chosen a domain name, which you will need to register with one of the domain companies. You can purchase it for one year upwards. While registering your domain, I would recommend the purchase of privacy protection as well. The price will be added to your domain cost. Privacy protection will hide your name and address from sellers and scammers. A friend's company had a website where their privacy was not protected. They received an email from a company in Europe, requesting a fee for their domain to be placed on the European registrar. They did not have to do this, but they were uncertain since everything about the email looked legitimate. It was easier to pay out the money than figure out if they really needed to. If your details are hidden, it will help prevent you from getting caught out.

As I've mentioned, your website should be an extension of your book. If your book is professional in look, your website needs to be also.

Your homepage, the page where initial visits happen, is the most important. It must draw the eye. Within that page should be links to everything on your site. An author contacted us recently requesting a review of his website. Hey had just launched his book. After several minutes of browsing the site, clicking into several pages, the book was nowhere to be found. Yet, in his defence, he could find it. He knew the maze of clicks to get to it - but no one else did.

From reading your book, to visiting your website, to anything you do, you must always anticipate customers' interaction. Pretend you're an outside visitor to your site: look for mistakes and changes that are needed. Ask a few people to check it out and report back to you.

If you have only one book, you don't need to set up a whole shopping site or the shopping page will look too empty. Create one web page that promotes your book, linked from your homepage. If you don't have much to say about yourself or your book, then place everything on your homepage. You can promote FREE CHAPTERS of your book available in PDF format. This allows people a glimpse into your book. The last page should have a BUY NOW button on it. This link should take them to your shopping cart. As building a website is beyond the scope of this book, I recommend a search on the internet for help in creating a site; or contact our website development team.

Good and bad reviews?

Don't put your faith in reviews unless they are numerous or the company has been recommended by someone you know that has used them. Some companies pay for reviews, and if the reviewer writes a positive review; they receive a free gift or payment. Would you trust those reviews?

I know a small business in Northern Ireland that specialises in a certain product that has only 4-6 customers per year. These customers have to visit the company's premises, pay a deposit, then pay the balance on receipt of their product. An unknown person from a small country far away, posted a Google review on the business. It stated that 'the product was sub-standard.' As the company has a record of all visits to their premises, they know this person has never been one of their customers. Yet, here we have someone from far off, and with no connection, trying to mischievously and negatively impact a business they never visited. So be discerning about what reviews you pay heed to.

A book trailer…

Digital content is universal now with smartphones, computers, etc. A generation around us is into apps, and the latest games that resemble Hollywood movies. To reach them, a slick video trailer is required. This is not just useful for YouTube: it can be placed on your website and social media platforms, as well as being shown to groups via a large screen, etc. In 2-3 minutes, a video trailer will grab the viewers' attention, and potentially sell your book.

Sometimes people can feel awkward trying to sell their book. I know experienced ministers that find it difficult to present their book for sale, in case people 'think' they are in it for the money. A video trailer[2] will present the book for them, removing that obstacle, letting them focus on the message. Also the video trailer can be sent to friends, and in turn can be shared through their social media outlets.

[2] *Visit Maurice Wylie Media on YouTube to see different book trailers.*

Accounts...

Before your book is released, visit a good accountant, and a benefits office if you are on benefits. Profits from the book sales will need to be declared as part of your income. Don't make any hasty decisions until you see income coming in. Don't leave your job or end benefits prematurely, etc. At this point, all you're doing is finding direction for *'what ifs.'* As Scripture states, *'My people are destroyed for lack of knowledge,'* Hosea 4:6. Don't let the lack of knowledge negatively impact your future.

Royalties...

Most book publishers provide royalties (a percentage of profit from the sale of your book). Yet, there are some who do not provide royalties to the author. They may either keep them, or pay them to the writer. Make sure you read the small print carefully.

Publishers can set targets for your royalties. On a traditional publishing contract, there is a set number of sales, e.g. '10,000 copies before you receive a royalty.' The majority of authors will not sell 10,000 copies. Another contract will be where you pay the publisher a fee to publish your book. This is more common for unknown authors. After paying the fee, they could either (1) still have a set number of sales to achieve before any royalty is paid, or (2) with or without a sales threshold, pay on average 8%-10% royalty. At Maurice Wylie Media we pay 30%+ royalty from the first book sold.

Don't be misled into thinking that when a publisher offers you a higher percentage royalty that you are making more money. This is not the case, for it means they are not making as much profit on your book, therefore, they won't be putting as much into promotion to sell more of your books.

All royalties are paid through your publisher, except if you have self-published, in which case you will have to chase the sales yourself. Publishers will normally pay once a year; but some pay every six months, as we do.

Royalty example...

Let's say your book sells at £10 (for easy counting) in retail.

Suppose the book costs £2.50 to print (depending on the size of book). That leaves £7.50 to be divided. The bookshop will require anything from 35%-65% depending on quantity. For this instance, let's say the shop is receiving 65% discount because they've ordered 1,000 copies. This means the bookshop will make £6.50 on the book. This would leave £1 profit to be split between the author and publisher.

In our royalty of 30%, the author would receive at least 30p and we the publisher would receive 70p to pay for postage, administration, and promotion of the book.

For wholesalers, the discount margins are higher than shops, but in turn they will buy larger quantities and so reduce the print costs.

Royalties can be lucrative, but only where there are large sales quantities involved. Think of the publishers who give 8% royalty to you. In the same example above, that would mean instead of your receiving 30p; you would receive only 8p.

Where possible, DIRECT SALES is the best to make the most profit. This is where you sell directly to customers via your website, bookstands, events, etc.

Important read...

I may need to emphasise the fact that the publisher cannot give 100% royalty to you. Not all bookshops - including Christian bookshops - want to pay the publisher for the books they have sold. I personally oversaw a transaction of three book orders with a Christian bookshop. The first order sold within a week, so another order was despatched. It also sold. Twenty days later, another order was delivered to their shop. After their 30 days of credit had expired, no payment had been received. An email was sent, phone calls were made, as well as a visit to the shop, but no payment was received for the books they sold. That was three years ago. The shop is still trading. I'm sure they have to pay their utility bills on time; but just because a shop takes your books, doesn't guarantee you'll receive payment. The slight profit we make from sales, then, has to go towards subsidising these unprofitable sales. I wish I could inform you that this practice is confined to one shop: unfortunately, it's not.

Where possible, give more discount to receive payment upfront. This will save time, hassle, and at least you will have made profit.

SOR...

Otherwise known as 'Sale or Return,' is something shops will push for. But SOR could take away their incentive to sell your book. It makes it easy for them to add your books to the others on display without risk. Why? Because the book has not cost them any money. When you sign up for SOR read the small print. It usually states that you will only receive payment if they sell your books - that's if you're able to prove they sold them.

There's another negative side to SOR. If you leave in five books and one book is sold, the other four could be in danger of shop damage

– normal wear and tear from people flicking through it. Or if one goes missing from the shelf, it is you who has to bear the cost, not the shop. Now can I ask: is it really such a good deal for you? Money up front is always better. A small profit is better than no profit. You'll still have to pay for your printing costs, delivery and time.

Self-Publisher's distribution and requirements...

One of our divisions helps people who seek to self-publish. Simply put, we craft the book and make it ready for publishing. The author then can place it directly onto Amazon, and in turn they can deliver it around the world. When your book is sold off Amazon, you'll receive payment each month. Our authors can place the book directly onto Amazon, but other publishers will not allow this. Our thinking is, it's never about who is selling the book, it's about selling the book; attaining sales.

When shops stock your books, they more than likely won't automatically send you any monies owed to you.

Self-publishing requires you to become a chaser...

You may think the first job of a chaser is to chase after money by emails, phone calls, calling into the shops in person requesting your money: but this is secondary.

Your first job a chaser is to record, record, record. You need to record what shops, churches, etc. have taken your books. Keep a sticky pad beside your phone, notepad in your car, etc. When the order is placed, then you can note the information.

These are the details you need to record…

Shop Name
Address
Buyer name
Telephone
Email
Date of order
Date of delivery
Book title (you may have more than one book)
Payment terms (SOR/Days of credit)
Quantity
Agreed discount
Balance
P & P
Total owed

Create an Excel report and always remember to back it up!

SAMPLE

SHOP NAME	GOSPEL WHOLESALE	MANNA STORE
ADDRESS	10 HIGH ST, LONDON	58 WEST ST, BELFAST
BUYER	JOHN JOHNSON	GRACE WATSON
TELEPHONE	0186 34 89 25	07901 757 545
EMAIL	buyer@gospel.com	grace@mannastore.com
DATE OF ORDER	03.03.21	05.05.21
DATE OF DELIVERY	03.04.21	05.05.21
TITLE	THE CHURCH	WALKING WITH GOD
PAYMENT TERMS	30 DAYS	60 DAYS
QUANTITY	100	1,000
AGREED DISCOUNT	30%	45%
BALANCE	£700	£5,500
P & P	£25	FREE
TOTAL OWED	£725	£5,500

Show your best side with debt...

When you chase your money, (as it will happen) telephone or email a week before it's due, just to see if everything is okay, you might ask if they need more books, and remind them of the payment. Don't be afraid to ask. Understand, based on your agreement, what is yours by agreement. In the buyer agreeing that everything is fine and you'll receive your money at the agreed time, then you know if your money does not arrive that, 'their word is questionable.' When you phone them to chase the money again, you cannot take their word at face value. This is where plan B comes into play.

Plan B1... Road trip!

Make a telephone call and find out from the person that keeps breaking their promises, what day they are in the shop. Then tell them the news that they have been eagerly waiting to hear; "I am in your area that day, and I will call to collect the monies owed to me." You'll likely smile at the other end of the phone when you hear their voice change.

Plan B2... Surprise, surprise...

If they are too far away and you cannot make the road trip, then this is where this plan comes in. When you keep getting promises that they are going to pay you, or they say, "next time I am in your area I'll pay you"... you just reply... "When was the last time you used your credit/debit card? No matter what they say, inform them, "To help you make your payment I have secured a card payment machine, and I can take that payment over the phone now for you!"

Plan B is challenging the person who does not want to be honest with you. Yet obviously when they have a genuine reason, like a family member has died, or Covid-19 has closed their shop temporarily, it's time to pour out grace and genuine concern. As a follower and representative of Jesus, showing love and compassion always has priority.

Book transportation...

It has been said that we at Maurice Wylie Media, work differently from normal Christian publishers. The objective of a publisher is to publish a book. But because we specialise in publishing inspirational stories, branding and websites, then we are committed, even after the book has been launched, to continue to partner with our authors. We promote them further with events, radio and television interviews (we're setting up our own television studio), and other opportunities to get their story out. And we try to help with the logistics when an author is travelling and speaking, and needs to have a steady supply of books available wherever he or she goes.

Suppose one of our local authors from Northern Ireland was visiting the USA or Australia for example, on a speaking tour. If they were to carry a suitcase of books to the event, it would cost them more than the books were worth. In a case like this, we work out a plan as follows:

When one of our author's travels abroad, for convenience, we arrange to have their books delivered in advance to the address where they are staying. We will arrange to have their books printed in the country or state they're visiting. If they're travelling across states in the US, we can have a batch of books waiting for them at their latest location. This takes away their concern as to whether the books are going to arrive undamaged, and it saves an international shipping cost.

Final stages of your book…

At the final stage you should have a PDF of your manuscript, allowing you to finalise each chapter, ensuring that paragraphs are spaced as necessary, and the text laid out as good as it can be.

The cover should be finished including the blurb. Both are extremely important to help sell your book. The copyright statements and any disclaimers are in place. You will have attained a nicely worded Foreword, from as well-known a person as you can find. Introduction and any dedications are written. Now that you know the number of pages that your book will comprise, this also gives you an idea of RRP. (Recommended Retail Price) Never overprice, or you will sell less. You're always better selling more, because the more people reading it, the more will talk about it, and that's FREE advertising. I know a person who self-published his autobiography. Even though his book was a powerful story of what God had done in his life, it was priced too high, making sales practically non-existent. We normally try to price our books under £10/$14.99, as people find it easier to part with ten pounds than twelve pounds.

You need to have decided whether your book is softback or hardback. We would always recommend softback. We only recommend hardback for personal copies or memoirs; hardback is usually twice the price, therefore fewer sales.

Never be too old to learn something new.

CHAPTER 7
It's Time for a Book Launch!

Some will ask, "Can I have more than one book launch?" The answer is "Yes!" Have as many as you like. It's your book, and you can do with it what you wish.

Allow three months to organise a book launch. The very minimum we have worked with is three weeks, but this is more workable if one has experience; the right connections, and a crowd already willing to come. Here's how it works:

1. Have a planning team. This will help you not to miss out on anything. The team may consist of your husband/wife only, friends, family, etc., but if possible, try and add someone who is a professional or at least competent into the team. You will find that they will look at things through a different set of eyes, and this will help balance the style of the launch.

2. Set your first meeting together as a planning team. Remember to keep everyone focused. They are there to get a job done. After the actions are discussed, they can then talk about anything else.

3. Keep notes on the meeting. Don't get side-tracked with other ideas that people may suggest.

4. Discuss where the book launch is to be. If you are involved with a church or a group, depending on how influential you are, you may get permission to hold your launch on the same night as some other event. If on average, 50 people are attending that meeting, you'll have 50 potential attendees for your event.

Some event locations for book launches:

Cafes
Churches
Shopping centres
Coffee shops
Craft fairs
Christmas events
Book events
Schools
Charity events (make a donation)
Conferences
Libraries
Museums

The most important groups are the groups you're already associated with; build from them.

5. Capacity is important to your chosen location. If you have a room with 100 seats and 100 people turn up, everyone will be talking about the packed house, which is a good advertisement. If the same 100 people turn up and your room has 300 seats, it won't have the same impact. You want to estimate the turnout by those you can depend on to come, plus the number that are expected at the other event, and then add another 20-30% seats. It's better to have people standing than have empty seats around the room.

6. Sales: We work mainly in two seasonal markets, Easter and Christmas. If you have a war story or 'armour of God' theme, this is the sort of book we would release for the Easter market. Christians tend to be up for a fight then, because of Jesus' victory over death.

7. Autobiographies, poetry, or books of love or similar topics, we usually release for the Christmas market. People love a good story to read right after Christmas day. Even though we can release books at any time, if we are releasing them for the Easter market, they will be in the shops at least 4-6 weeks before Easter. For the Christmas market they will be in the shops at the latest, eight weeks before Christmas. With our vast experience on book launches, we can tell you that if yours is done well, then on average you will sell one or two copies per person in attendance at Easter. For the same book launch happening at Christmas, you will sell three to five copies per person. Which one would you choose?

8. Decide on a date, but before you confirm it, check whether anything is happening in the area that might detract from your event. I know a guy who promoted his book launch, only to discover it was on Halloween night. He wasn't too concerned at first, but then he found out that the location he had booked was also running a Halloween event. I don't need to tell you how his event went.

9. Decide on who the host is, (not yourself) and whether you're having music/singing. Have some people talking about you and the book, like whoever wrote the Foreword. Sometimes we have had interviews with the author on the stage, or the author reading passages from the book, especially if it is poetry.

10. You will need posters designed. Your publisher may be able to do this for you, but there is normally a designer in every town. Site the posters around places in which there is a large footfall, otherwise they'll not be as effective. If it is a Christian book, ask churches whether you might put a poster up in their lobby. Ask the designer to scale a version down to A5, or even smaller. This can then be used in png format for your social pages.

11. By this stage you should have a growing number following you on your social pages. Now you can start inviting them to the launch by setting up an event on your page. People can click indicating they'll attend, though it's is easy for someone to do this and then change their mind, so don't be disappointed if they don't turn up.

12. A good way to thank people for coming to your book launch is to have food available. If your church is hosting it for you, often members will bring food with them, which reduces your overheads. Some launches will have a sit-down meal, but the majority will have a finger-buffet, or just tea/coffee and sandwiches. It all comes back to the type of crowd that is coming, and also your budget.

13. Pop-up banners for the book are a good idea and can be easily obtained. We would normally have two at the entrance (this simply lets people know where the door is, especially if you're in a hotel setting). We then put two on the platform. It adds a professional touch to the front, and reminds people why they are there. Lastly, and just as importantly, we have one or two at the book stand - not behind the book stand, but beside it. Why? Because people can take a selfie with the author and guess what? They are posting that to their timelines and hitting that share button-free advertising for you.

14. A nice, sharp display will help present your book properly. Set up the display table based on the number of people you're expecting at the event. For example, if there are 30 people in attendance, don't have 500 books displayed. Based on expected attendance, you should multiply it by 3 for display, and if need be, have another box of books under the table.

Purchase a simple table cover for each table you are using for the books to sit on. This will give your display a more professional look. If you want to go to a higher level, there are companies online that will print your table cover for you, and put your name/logo on it. If you're unsure what sheet colour to use, take some different colour cloths, towels, etc., and lay them down with your book on them. The colour that enhances your book is the one you should use.

DISPLAY! DISPLAY! DISPLAY! They say a picture is like a thousand words; your book display is your picture! You may not think this important, but practise your display.

First, search the internet for 'book displays' or 'book tables' or similar. In these searches, you'll see how others set up their display. Then practise setting up yours.

At this point, you can use your kitchen table. Put your sheet over it (it does not need to be ironed at this point, but it will for your official launch). The reason you're putting the sheet on now is to make sure the colour enhances your books, especially if you have several titles. The wrong colour will take away from them.

We use professional book stand holders that can keep two to three books upright at a time, for the rear of the display. You could also use an old wooden crate, as long as it complements the display, it might even make it look more interesting. Then you can set five to eight books on top of each other, with one at the front of the stack. You could potentially have several piles on the table. Place your leaflets and your business cards carefully. You never know: someone might ask you to help them write their book. Another source of income!

Once you get the display all set up, count the books displayed and take a photo of it. That photo is your display layout. Put everything on display into boxes and mark boxes as DISPLAY: this is what you will use for future reference. After each sale event, re-stock the boxes to the number you had. Now you're ready for your next event.

If the next event is larger, you just need to add another box or two, but remember to do the same thing again: practise the display. This will save you time at the event. You will know exactly where everything is, how many books per stack, etc.

If your book represents a certain topic, e.g. football; then have a football on the stand. It will just add more life to it. You never know; people might end up talking about the props on your stand more than your book; at least they're talking! Stay focused, though: the goal is to sell books, not promote props.

RESEARCH! RESEARCH! RESEARCH! Never be slack in doing your homework: it will save you time and money. When you have secured an event; check to see if they can provide tables, a projector for PowerPoint if you use a laptop, and electronic payments if you use internet. Find out how close the boxes of books can get to their display location. You don't want to be walking a mile back and forth with 48 books in a box. See how close your car or lorry can get to where the book table will be; what time you will need to be there to allow set up before people arrive. Depending on distance, you may require a trolley to move the boxes of books, or even a helper.

15. Cash is king, they say! Remember to carry a float, keeping change. If your book is £9.99, make sure you have quite a few pennies, as some will ask for the penny change. It is the same with any other currency. In this age, card payments are also essential. It used to be one would have to commit to paying monthly charges for this service whether a sale was made or not. However, there are now card merchants that will provide you with the card machine for a small fee, and there are no monthly payments. Like an online shop, they will take a percentage of the transaction (average 2%).

Strange as it may sound, not everyone will come to your book launch with money. Having some leaflets printed promoting your book, directing them to your website, etc., will help to retain a sale for those who want to buy a book, but haven't brought cash or a card. At times like this, we will issue our authors with a website code which gives the purchaser FREE postage. This means they are getting the book at the same price as if they had purchased it at the launch.

You may be concerned that the author is now having to pay for the postage out of the book profits. Yes, this is true. In the United Kingdom the average cost for book postage is £1.50. That means £1.50 will be removed from the profit of that book. But focus on the fact that you have made a sale which you may not otherwise have had. Also, the person who is now reading your book could be a walking advertisement for your book. And depending on its content, their life might be changed for the better, while you still made a considerable profit.

16. Don't forget to inform the babysitter that you'll be home very late – maybe the early hours of the morning. You could be the first one in and the last one out for the launch.

If you have something important the following day, make sure as much of that is done before you go to your book launch.

17. Do you have a doctor signature or schoolboy signature? Practise a 'book signature.' Note: I did not state, 'your own signature!' If you use your regular signature, it's a security risk. If a scammer were able to obtain your financial details, knowing what your signature looked like would increase their chances of accessing your bank accounts. Design what I call a book signature, and practise it numerous times. Don't worry if you don't get it 100% every time; the acknowledgement is you writing on the book. Remember to ask who it should be signed to, and, "is it for something special?" You can sign off then with both your name and a meaningful phrase or a verse of Scripture.

Example

To Audrey,

Wishing you a Happy Birthday

M Wylie

Phil. 3:13-14

> "
>
> There are a thousand opportunities on the hills for you to prosper in God.

CHAPTER 8
Time to Turn up the Heat...

Unless your book is going to uncover some great revelation, then it is an upward struggle to gain exposure through newspapers, television, or radio, except by paid advertising. But don't give up: good advice is at hand.

National newspapers will only have articles that they deem of interest to their readership on a national scale. We have had our main national newspapers in Northern Ireland run front-page news on several of our authors, but the key is to use your local newspaper if you don't have access to the nationals. And the good news is that the national newspapers will be combing local newspapers for news that may interest them. For now, let's focus on getting your book into your local newspaper for FREE.

I know you'll likely think this goes without saying as it is common sense, but an extremely important fact about local newspapers is - they want only LOCAL NEWS. Anything beyond that doesn't interest them. So, the way to get yourself into your local newspaper is - by becoming local!

For example, where you live qualifies you for local news in that area. But also, where were you originally from? That qualifies you for that area. And then where is your office? That might be a different location? We ask these questions to our authors, and in turn, we use their locations for local newspapers. On top of that, we use our publisher locations to make entrance into those local newspapers.

You can search the internet for newspaper email addresses, editor names, phone numbers, etc. Do not send in a letter via post. Today's media is all about speed. You can write to them via a word document attached to your email, or within the email itself. Here is a sample of how we release news to a newspaper and media outlets:

SAMPLE ONE: LOCAL NEWSPAPER

PRESS RELEASE
DATE

#START#

LONDON BOOK LAUNCH FOR LOCALLY BASED PUBLISHER

A local base publishing company is going from strength to strength with their latest publication children's brand, 'Spottea & Dottea Travels.'

Following their successful launch at Bantry Literary Festival, West Cork, 'Maurice Wylie Media,' run by Maurice Wylie, will now travel to London to launch the second book in the series.

'Spottea & Dottea Travels' series has been designed for those years of understanding, and according to the feedback Maurice Wylie Media is receiving, children and adults alike are loving it.

The spokesperson continued: *"With the second book nearly ready, we have been invited to London for the launch of it. Churches and retailers are registering their interest in attending this event, and according to reports, it could be a night to remember."*

"With the popular Christian magazine and several radios stations running interviews, it looks bright for this summer!"

More details can be obtained from their website, www.MauriceWylieMedia.com or contacting them on telephone number 0845 000 000

#END#

(Write-up has been condensed for the purpose of highlighting main points)

Dear Editor,

Please see the above article made ready for submission. If you require any further information, I'll be happy to provide it.

Your name
Mobile number
Email address

Attached
Photo 1 – Name of your book
Photo 2 – Name of author

SAMPLE TWO: NATIONAL NEWSPAPER

PRESS RELEASE
DATE

#START#

PUBLISHER DRAWS TV AUDIENCE

Maurice Wylie Media has drawn the attention of Revelation TV with their new book, 'The Good, The Bad & Jesus Christ' by Pastor James McConnell.

Over the last few months their publishing and design teams have been preparing the ground for the new book release.

The senior presenter of Revelation TV will be filming a live interview with Pastor McConnell and other guest speakers during the launch night.

Speaking with their senior presenter, he said: *"We have a large TV audience throughout the UK and Europe. When we heard of such a book being published, we knew our audience would be very interested in it."*

The book has already received pre-orders and with them comes a signed copy. Purchasers will receive them immediately after the book launch.

As the author is known to be the greatest evangelist in the 20th century in Ireland, this book will enlighten and inspire, and is expected to be a best-seller!

#END#
(Write up has been condensed to highlight main points)

Dear Editor,

Please see the above article made ready for submission. If you require any further information, I'll be happy to provide it.

Your name
Mobile number
Email address

Attached
Photo 1 – Name of your book
Photo 2 – Name of author

Review those two write-ups and note the locations; each one used to enter a local newspaper.

As you read through it, every paragraph is designed to create interest and draw in the reader.

While your book and the above thoughts are fresh in your mind, why don't you write out the bones of your press release in your notebook or below:

YOUR NEWSLETTER TEMPLATE

HEADING:

First paragraph

List 5-10 points you wish the people to know?

1
2.
3.
4.
5.
6.
7.
8.
9.
10.

Either go to the back of the book or use another item to write your storyline connecting the points you want them to know. Check it against the sample listed previously to make sure all angles are covered.

The power of sharing on social platforms…

With the social media platforms having such an influence, especially among the younger generation; you MUST accept that social media can be a useful tool if operated correctly.

By now you should have a following; no matter if it's a few or thousands of followers or friends, the key is: put yourself in front of them! This is done by sharing: for example, the cover of your book; statements from your book; a picture of yourself; some details of the writing journey; all this and more can be shared.

Share through FACEBOOK LIVE. With Facebook Live, people can interact with you and ask you questions, etc. Above all, ask them to share. StreamYard is a good system to use.

Three aspects of sharing…

Organic – It just happens naturally. People see your posts and share them.

After shares – Someone has shared your post to their own page. One of their friends, connected to them but not to you, then shares that same post.

(Note that in order for your posts to be shared from one person to another, you have to set your privacy settings to 'Public,' not just 'Friends.')

Paid – You can select a paid advertisement through social media. When you create your advert, it will allow you to choose the demographics for people seeing your advert; male or female; religion; employment, income, etc.

> *Never accept that just because someone has a title, they are good at their job.*

CHAPTER 9
Self-Publishing VS Publisher!

In recent years, self-publishing has rocketed. In my opinion, people want to take advantage of the opportunity to have a book published, without having to suffer rejection and have their fate decided by the big publishers. Digital technology has made self-publishing feasible, so that now, the author can make the decisions and potentially more profit into the bargain. But they do need to work harder to make it happen.

Self-publishing isn't easy if you're trying to do it all on your own. You will either have to take on the following roles, or commission third parties to handle them for you.

Self-publishing

You MUST do the following:

- Authoring (that's your job!)
- Copy-editing
- Book formatting (e-book and print)
- Cover designing
- Email list: building blocks
- Finance
- Advertising creative
- Advertising monitoring and adjustment
- Structural editing
- Proofreading
- Copywriting
- Website construction
- Email list: copy
- Advertising strategy
- Legal protection

Traditional Publishing

PUBLISHER DOES IT ALL

One serious issue that lies with self-publishing versus a publisher is the legal protection, especially under the subsidiary rights (Explained earlier).

I knew a person who self-published. His book sold very well due to its content. A Hollywood producer heard about it and made a film based on the guy's book. The film was a hit. How much money did he receive from the movie? A BIG ZERO.

He had no traceability to the story (yet he was the story) and no legal protection. Any publisher worth their salt will have good protection if such a thing should happen to one of their authors. Self-publishing is great when you have everything in place, but what he lost was more than he ever gained.

SALES IS ONLY… Bringing people over a line!

Sales can be an uphill struggle, especially from the mindset of Christians; when you mention sales. Immediately they think: 'Promotion, pride, money, etc. Surely, it cannot be right?'

Yet, everything we do in life relates to selling. Oh, we may not use that word, but it is true!

From the first time you went out on an official date, I am sure you washed, made sure you smelled good and thought about what clothes to wear. What were you doing? You were selling!

When you visit a supermarket, a lot of research has gone into where to place items in the shop. What are they doing? They are selling!

That tin of soup is squealing itself off the shelf: BUY ME! If you listen carefully, they never play fast music. You know why? They don't want you speeding up around the aisles.

When you go to church on Sunday and time has been spent presenting everything properly, from the music, to the preaching; what are they doing? (I know I'm going to get into trouble for this but), they are selling! But before you stone me (!) let's understand the meaning of 'selling.' The most common definition of the word is: **'to exchange for money.'** But did you know it also means: **'persuade someone of the merits of?'**

It is like when you have a child not eating their food, and you play the pretend aeroplane with the spoon, making the noise of it flying the food the whole way into the child's mouth. What are you doing… you're selling! You're making something cross over a line: in this case, food!

Outreach for any church is a sales platform for that church or for Jesus Christ. We sell the gospel. Okay, we don't exchange money for it, but the whole purpose of outreach is to bring people across a line, whether that is for conversation, attending church, or, more importantly, committing their lives to Jesus. We are bringing them over the line.

Think! What was it that brought you over the line to purchase this book? Are you able to write up to three answers?

1.	
2.	
3.	

Let me ask you: have you got any of those three things in your book?

BOOKS! BOOKS! BOOKS!

All this can be exhausting; but learn to chill, or as we say, "Take a chill pill!" (time out)

LEARN TO CELEBRATE NOW – NOT LATER!

If you wait until the war of sales is over, you'll not enjoy the ride, the success, and the achievements that you have made.

Scripture says, *'Do not despise these small beginnings, for the LORD rejoices to see the work begin.'* Zechariah 4:10 NLT. Did you read that? Even the LORD rejoices to see a work begin, and we are urged not to despise what is small in our eyes.

When I started writing my first book, the whole goal was to get it finished, get it published, and see lives changed and so forth. But in reality (even though God spoke to me through the writing of it) I never fully appreciated the 'process of the journey,' as in, 'WOW THIS IS GOOD, THIS IS AN ACHIEVEMENT.'

Learn to CELEBRATE when you have a creative direction for your book, or for that idea, etc. I'm not saying you need to drop everything and go and hold a party every time. Just pat yourself on the back and say: 'that was good!' Take a deep breath and off to work again: now write.

When you finish that first chapter, when you complete the book, when you receive your first sale: Learn to celebrate!

My second book sold out at the first conference I was speaking at. On the way home, God was saying to me; "Celebrate!" whereas all I was thinking about was the fact that money from the sales had to go back to order more books. Yet, God was saying; "Celebrate!" I don't believe God was saying to celebrate because all the books sold; but it was the first event, and it was an achievement. Do you not think your heavenly Father celebrates with you, like a natural father would? That night on my way home, I stopped at a garage, opened the money float, took out money, went into the garage and purchased a bar of chocolate. Then I sat in the car and ate it, putting the change back in the float. Yes; at that moment, achievement was (and always is) important. The only difference from then until now is that I ate the chocolate not really wanting it, because I wanted to save all the money. Now, I celebrate achievements that God gives me. I take my wife out for dinner, buy her flowers, etc. Yes, even our achievement does not have to be about us; it can be about those who have stood with us.

We encourage our authors to celebrate the moment. Even now I need to pause in what I am doing to go and collect an author that's just launched his new book with us. He doesn't know that his books are now in the shops. I will take him into the shop and surprise him. I can't wait to see his face. That's an achievement – his book in shops! If he behaves, I might buy him a coffee, and we'll talk about the journey. LIVE THE MOMENT – CELEBRATE!

DON'T JUST AIM STRAIGHT AHEAD, AIM WIDE...

We can be so focused only on the printed book that we miss other great opportunities. It is not just about the printed book; it is about the message of the book. And with that you then extend it into the following:

E-BOOK OR PRINTED BOOK?

People have asked me which book they should produce: an e-book or a printed book?

My answer has always been the same: a printed book **with** an e-book. You see, it takes nearly the same amount of work to create a printed book as it does to make an e-book.

You'll still need your editor, proofreader, typesetter, designer, etc. Okay, you may not need a back cover for your e-book, but all in all, the printed book will outsell the e-book hands down.

The Association of American Publishers annual report for 2019, says that books in all formats made almost $26 billion in revenue last year in the US, with print-making up $22.6 billion and e-books $2.04 billion. Those figures include trade and educational books, as well as fiction.

Software that can read your manuscript is easily accessible, and you can make it into an e-book if you have basic computer knowledge.

Ebook platforms…

Amazon has over 300 million readers. Smashwords, Google Play, and similar platforms are now available. As an e-book publisher, we host our e-books on over 70 platforms worldwide.

Most e-book platforms will pay on average 50% royalty on every sale of your e-book. Do remember that, due to the book being digital, there are normally VAT charges on each sale, reducing your profit.

Ebook or audio book?

The Audio Book Market is projected to grow at a rate of 27.0% in terms of value, from 2019, to reach USD 19.39 billion by 2027. The global audiobook market is currently undergoing enormous growth. Many consumers are becoming more inclined to listen to the audible version of books, novels, and poetry.

The Association of American Publishers (AAP) released their report of 2018 stats on revenue for consumer book publishers. A StatShot report, said that revenue for three book categories (Adult Books, Children's/Young Adults, and Religious Presses) saw growth, and the $7.9 billion from 2018 was a 4.6 % increase over 2017.

The most noticeable increase was in audiobook sales, jumping by 37.1%, an additional $127.1 million since 2017. The AAP, notes that downloaded audio (as opposed to physical audiobook formats) has been the format with the most growth since 2013. "This is the third consecutive year that audiobooks saw double-digit growth (+37.1%) and eBook revenue declined (-3.6%)," the AAP report says.

They believe the growth in sales is because people want to pack more into their available time. With a set of earphones and the audiobook playing, they can still be gardening, working, running, etc.

With the majority of people having access to computers with a microphone, or smartphones, some authors will record their own audiobook. A voice recording has the potential to help sell your book. But it needs the right delivery. A voice that's monotonous and without passion, or that just sounds unprofessional, may put people off rather than encourage them to buy or recommend.

Television talent shows are about finding talent; but they usually also let people hear those who can't sing, but, sad to say, who believe they can. It's the same with the Audio Book: If your own voice isn't going to do your book justice, then choose someone who has the required level of professionalism to give your project credibility. The voice must do you justice.

With our soon to be launched studio; we will be able not just to record the reader, but also enhance the recording with music and effects. If anything is worth doing, it is worth giving it your best.

What you don't want to read, but need to...

Just because a publisher or bookshop claims they are Christian, does not mean they adhere to Christian values.

A minister once introduced me to a member of his church who had had a book published by a Christian publisher. The author showed me his book, which looked reasonable. I asked, was he happy with the finished product? He said, "I likely would have been, but quite a number of pages are not mine, and yet I had no say in the matter." The publisher had added more content to fill out the book so that it could attract a higher selling price. Another publisher enlarged the text and added double spacing between the lines. Why? To enlarge the book and charge more. I am personally opposed to tactics like these.

The MWM process on grounds of acceptance is as follows:

- We review your content.
- Decide whether we can proceed to next stage.
- Send proposal to author.
- Agreement signed.
- Work with author to produce manuscript thoroughly.
- Creative team produces concept, title, etc.
- Appoint one or several of our cover designers.
- We edit the manuscript using three benchmarks: concept, spiritual, life-changing.
- Review by proofreader.
- Blurb created.
- Quality control: reviewed again with team and author.
- Author signs off / gives permission.
- Book published.

> *What you don't know, you will not see.*

CHAPTER 10
Fast Track Development...

What do I write about? Write about something you enjoy!

Q. What do you enjoy?

___

Q. What three words describe me?

___

Q. What's the most unusual thing about me?

___

Q. My greatest strength is?

___

Q. My greatest weakness is?

___

Q. I'm most afraid of?

___

Q. What book have you enjoyed reading?

___

Q. What was it that you enjoyed the most about it?

___

Q. If it was your birthday and you had three wishes, what would they be?

___

Q. Eventually, my ambition is to?

___

HOW TO CREATE A CHARACTER...

Think about people or animals that you know. Reflect on their appearance, their hopes, and their bad habits.

Write these here

Bad Points   Good Points

Reviewing what you've written down; which of these points would you like your new character to have in them?

I would like my character A to have
_____

I would like my character B to have
_____

And so on.

BOOK STAGES...

Good carving presents food; good editing presents impressive storylines.

We specialise in autobiographies, and in them we seek to carve a storyline in such a way that it has been known for readers to have burned their dinners, due to being so engrossed in the book. The following is about the fullness of the book, more than how we would carve each chapter.

Stage 1

The BEGINNING
(The main character is introduced, and the scene is set.)

Who is/are the main character/s?
Where are the main locations for the setting?

Stage 2

The BUILD-UP
(Something happens that changes the hero's situation.)

What happens to get your story started?
What brings the characters together?

Stage 3

The CLIMAX
(The main character confronts a big problem.)

What will be the main problems your characters have to deal with?
How do these problems link?

Stage 4

The RESOLUTION
(The problem is resolved in some way.)

How does your character resolve the situation?
How does the resolution flow from the climax?

Stage 5

The END
(The loose ends of your story are tied up and you show how things have changed for your character since the start.)

What way do you want the reader to feel at the end of your story?
What way will you finish the story to make your reader feel like that?

> *Sales is only... bringing people over a line.*

CHAPTER 11
Avoid Costly Mistakes!

I can tell you right up front; mistakes will happen, and the higher your quality of production/content, the more efforts and filters you need to put in place.

Here are some keys to help prevent mistakes:

Children's book with illustrations…

Check to see what age group you are writing for and make sure the illustrations align to the age group. Not only then do you need to check the grammar/storyline, but you need to make sure that each character that you've included stays within their character/dress code, hairstyle etc.

Within this book, you will find sections under, *'How to Create a Character' & 'Writing a Fiction Book.'* Please use whichever one is the most suitable for you. Check and double-check that you stay within the parameters of your description for each character.

Most author's love their own manuscript and they are happy when they receive praise for it. But remember, an honest critic will highlight what they see. Don't take their criticism to heart, instead, understand that they want the best for you. If you want honest feedback, then consider getting it from one of the best sources – children.

Just because you like your own book does not mean to say children will like it. Print off some pages of the book, even several books and then go to your local school and ask the children to be involved. Ask them what they like and don't like. Watch their expressions. Are they drawn in or uninterested? This is vital feedback, and don't be standing defending the book; let them speak.

I have seen one of our children's authors stand in front of 200 children, and you could hear a pin drop as she read from her book. That type of response is what you are looking for. It sets the bar as to what to expect when the book goes on sale.

Reprints…

If you're a self-publisher, place a small code on the back cover of your first print. It is not the first time someone has printed hundreds or thousands of books and then discovered a mistake. They then make corrections and do a second, third, or fourth print run just to get it right. Soon your garage or spare room is full of books, including the corrected ones. But now you can't tell which ones are which - they all look the same. The code, however, will keep you right should this mix-up ever occur.

Writing a fiction book…

Create a character for each person within your script, then print off the name of the character with all their characteristics. For example:

Name
Nicknames
Height
Body size
Colour of skin
Body features (tattoos)
Dress code – old jeans, sweater too big, bright colours
Attitude – Short temper, needs to smell fresh, nerd, and so on.

As you write your story, then you know who to bring into it and how to tie it together. Otherwise you will mix up the characters. Even though you know who you are writing about, the text could be confusing.

First delivery only happens once…

Where possible, you should always have your books delivered a few weeks before your book launch.
Be prepared for printing problems to happen. Parts of books can be printed wrongly; page edges ripped if printer is using a blunt guillotine; books in the boxes damaged during delivery, and that's only some of what can happen. If you keep a couple of spare weeks from delivery to launch it may just give you enough time to replace the books for the launch.

There was only one Elvis…

Do not pack your manuscript with details that are not important to the reader, even for an autobiography, unless your name is Elvis. The reader does not care how many houses you've moved to, and their addresses, what colour your parent's walls were, etc. Unless it's a history book, detailing certain events, then intrigue overrides detail.

Grammar vs culture…

As important as it is to have correct grammar, never prioritise culture over grammar. Each person or community has its own style of culture. Within that culture, they will have certain statements and a vocabulary within the communication that is taking place. How one communicates can bring a sparkle to your book. If you're writing a local book, use your local vernacular. We have published local books using a language style that means one thing locally and something totally different elsewhere. In situations like this, put the broader meaning into brackets beside your word or statement.

Don't rob the buyer…

Everything has a price; like certain sized bars of chocolate or daily newspapers, etc. They all sit within their own price margin. Imagine paying for a box of sweets and discovering half of them were missing. Or a number of pages are missing from the newspaper. Would you be happy? Because you thought you had purchased something for the price you paid, you expect the price you paid to deliver a certain standard. Always try to give value for money. Bad news travels a lot quicker than good news. Set aside that it is your book you are pricing; then ask, if this was someone else's book, is it worth the money? Price accordingly.

Don't be deceptive with space…

A blank page here, another one there, then another, and then: double spacing between the lines. What is the author/publisher doing? They are filling the book with empty space. Why? They are projecting that the book is worth more by making it appear bigger than the content justifies. They then set the price by the weight of paper, which is deceptive. People don't want to spend their money on blank paper. Ensure you give them valuable content or expertise.

THE LAST NOTE
Leave an inheritance...

I remember a person once challenged an author as to why he was selling his book for £20/$25. The author calmly responded, "I have spent the last 40 years learning, making mistakes, achieving results, making money, etc. What you have in your hand is the cream of that journey, the 'how not to' and 'how to.' What you have in your hand will save you thousands in mistakes and could even make you money. Now then, is £20/$25 good value for what I have given you?" The person answered, "yes!"

I pray that I have done justice to you investing your money into this book; that it was an investment more than an expense; that it has helped straighten the road that is ahead of you.

Some have asked, "why spend money on publishing a book when I can use it for a holiday?" For me, the answer is very simple. What holiday did you ever go on that you remember everything about? We remember the highlights or lowlights, but both are just *lights* in our mind. On each page of this book and others that I've written, I can tell you exactly what was happening, who I was thinking about, etc., just as your book will hold facts that you will always remember. And long after you and I are gone, and holidays all forgotten, someone will be reading my story. I hope they'll be reading your story also. You're not just investing in a book; you're investing in the life of all those who will be reading your book.

We have been honoured at Maurice Wylie Media that the majority of our books are now registered for protection under United Kingdom law. What does that mean? That means that long after you and I have left this earth, that generations to come will be able to read the work of the authors that we published, including this book.

My attitude is very simple in this matter. I can spend money on cars and holidays, and they'll never change a life. Or I can invest it in a book and know that one day in Heaven, someone will come through those gates to tell me, "Your book taught me about Jesus." A soul is surely worth every penny.

Have you ever noticed that God works from one generation to another, leaving an inheritance for His forthcoming generation? If God believes that it is important, then so must we through our faith in Him. Through this conviction, He motivates us to not just record the lives of living and past saints in God, but to make sure the future generation can also read about them.

I pray the words you've read in this book will help you get over any hurdle and fear. If you require help - we can journey together.

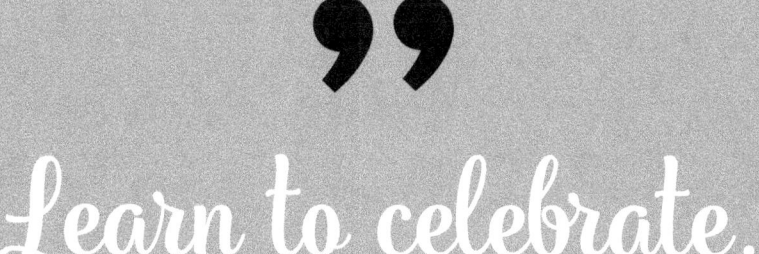

EXTRAS

SOFTWARE TO HELP YOU WRITE…

Microsoft Word www.Microsoft.com is the largest software platform for writing, and probably the most popular. However, it's not free, however, so you will either have to pay a monthly fee or buy a licence outright. You can transfer the licence to another computer.

Here are some free options…

Google Docs, www.Google.com If you have a Google account, you'll be able to use this software free of charge. One advantage is that you can save your work in Google's cloud and as long as you have your login details to the cloud you can access those files from another computer.

For just a word processor…

Apache OpenOffice Writer www.OpenOffice.org

LibreOffice Writer www.LibreOffice.org

WPS Office Writer www.PC.WPS.com

Microsoft Office Word Online www.Microsoft.com/en-us/microsoft-365/free-office-online-for-the-web is a free alternative to the paid version of Word: Office Online.

AUTHOR'S PLATFORM...

"Some years ago, I was challenged to write a book. When someone spoke to me about it, I said, "Oh no, my life is just a normal Christian life."

When I explained to them some of the things that I would put in my book, they said, "believe me this is not the normal Christian life; write your book.

So, I prayed and set about seeking to recall experiences that I could write about. I self-published a book with an American company, and it was a terrible experience.

However, when I felt moved to write a second book about my healing from Lymphoma, seemingly by accident, I found Maurice Wylie.

In my dealings with them I found them clear, honest, helpful, and it was a good experience which helped me orifice a book I'm pleased with."

Margaret Cornell, author of *Why Me God?* (England)

"When God spoke to me to write a book based on 2 Corinthians 10:4, it took me seven years to complete it, but when it was finally finished, I found myself asking, 'Now what?' I knew I needed help and direction. I am a preacher, not a writer. Some told me to self-publish, but I wanted it to be the best it could be. I concluded that I needed expert assistance. I knew my work required a lot of editing, so I contacted some of my preacher friends who had written books. My good friend and fellow pastor advised me to contact Maurice Wylie, and I did.

Maurice and his team treated me very professionally, taking away any concerns that I had, ensuring that the book would only be printed when I was happy with it. They looked over my manuscript, and the first thing they did was to explain that a lot of editing (confirming my concerns) is required to make the book more effective. Simply put, they revamped my manuscript. Throughout the whole process, Maurice was an encourager to me, and when I read over the book prior to the final draft and before publishing, I felt as if I was reading the work of a real pro! Maurice Wylie Media transformed my words into much more.

I wrote the book in obedience to the Lord, and hopefully to give the Body of Christ tools to equip saints to win Spiritual battles. I am thankful for Maurice Wylie and his team for making this dream become a reality."

Dr. Robert Ballard, author of *Strategic Spiritual Warfare* (USA)

"I felt that from the beginning of my book journey, Maurice Wylie and his team were there to support me. From the moment the seed of my story was planted, we had many discussions about every detail concerning the ideas and books. Maurice inspired and encouraged me, often making insightful suggestions which I weaved into the stories. I discussed every character with him and watched them come to life with his support. I believe that Maurice has a gift of discernment.

Maurice Wylie Media (MWM) also organised an illustrator for my books and sent me drawings to review. They listened to my input and asked my opinion at every stage. They organised my book launch, which for me was a dream come true. Once my first book, *Let the Adventures Begin*' was almost complete, the second one, *'The Valley of Decision*' was beginning to take shape in my mind and Maurice's. The same happened with the third, and now I have three stories forming the start of a children's book series.

I am looking forward to working with MWM again in the near future to publish the next story in the Spottea Dottea series. My two little ladybirds have more adventures to make as they travel through Scripture, bringing truth to life.

I would highly recommend Maurice Wylie Media and am forever grateful that our paths crossed at the right time, but that is a story for another day.

Melanie O'Sullivan, author of *Spottea & Dottea Travels* (Republic of Ireland)

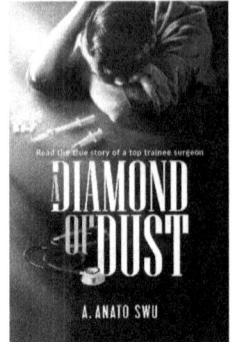

"I never thought or even dreamed that one day, my books would be published for international readership; and that too, by the reputed and inspirational Christian publisher, Maurice Wylie Media (MWM). But within a span of two years, I have had two books published by them.

I had already self-published my book, not realising the difference from what I had published to what MWM would do would be like night to day.

Over several years I had got then to know Maurice and Maureen Wylie and shared with Mama Maureen, my published book. In turn, she shared it with her husband, Maurice. It was then I learned that one day he lifted my self-published book and read through it. He said, "It was like a diamond covered in dust… and we can remove the dust and make it glitter as God would have intended."

What I thought in my book being finished and printed initially was only a draft compared to the finished book, *"A Diamond Of Dust."*

MWM promptly returned the manuscript with suggestions, pin-pointing changes, and to elaborate or strip it back where necessary. I was guided by their team in this new venture of writing. Likewise, my second book, *'The Dancing Quill'* was also published a year later.

Both of my books have been made possible because of the love and concern, and relentless effort of my now spiritual parents. Even the title of my books was given by them as per a God-given vision.

It did not just end with my books being published; it has opened many doors for me to share across the world. I am forever grateful that God connected me to these two-inspiring people.

A. Anato Swu, author, *A Diamond of Dust and The Dancing Quill*
(Nagaland, India)

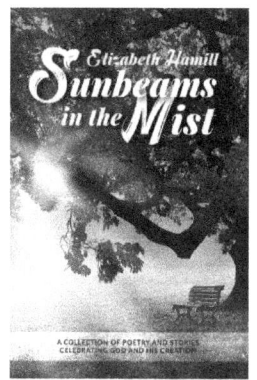
"My journey in writing started as a child… I added bits and pieces over the years, and it was in 1998/9 I decided to take the gigantic step of looking for someone to help me sort out the mountain of stories and poems I had accumulated over the years.

I knew nothing about anything to do with publishing! The search for a publisher [Christian] was difficult… weeks passed, and then I found via the internet, `Maurice Wylie Media`…; there was a contact phone number.

It took me two weeks before I had the courage to dial the number… fear of being laughed at; having no confidence, and being in the very mature age group are just a few of the reasons that kept me from making the call.

Finally, I made the call. A call that took me on a journey… the road had many ups, downs and bends, a few times I was on the point of giving up… it was the tremendous support I received from Maurice that kept me going.

The finished book was a delight to my eyes. Never in my wildest dreams did I envisage it complete; the cover, layout and the clear typeset was pleasing to the eye. Thank you, Maurice, and all the staff at Maurice Wylie Media. I pray that your book will help overcome the many fears, and answer the numerous questions that fit into the mind of a budding author.

Your book is a brilliant idea and one that will be appreciated by many budding authors."

Elizabeth Hamill, author, *Sunbeams in the Mist* (N. Ireland)

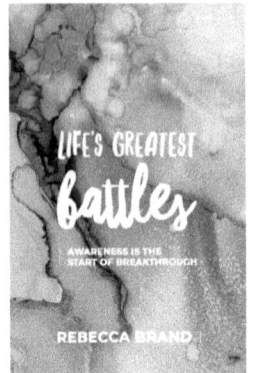

"Honestly, writing a book was the "easy" part, but the world of publishing is brutal! I was an unknown first-time author with a manuscript sat on my PC. I had a desire to see it published and a fire in my heart to push forward with the idea that "I could do this," but I had no idea what was next in the journey.

After speaking with well-known publishers, I decided that the "traditional publishing" route was not for me. Then I became even more disheartened after speaking to Self-Publishing companies...until I sent my manuscript to Maurice and his wonderful team.

Nothing was a burden for them, nor any question too small. They walked me through this unknown journey with such grace and wisdom that it didn't feel stressful or overwhelming at any stage. Thank you, team, for bringing my dream to life, and the reality of being a published author. I have seen my book reach places in the world that I didn't think possible, and I ended up with a book that has changed people's lives, and that ultimately, I am proud of. I wouldn't use any other publishing team!"

Rebecca Brand, Conference Speaker and author, *Life's Greatest Battles* **(New Zealand)**

> The voice must do you justice.

INSPIRED TO WRITE A BOOK?

Contact
Maurice Wylie Media
Your Inspirational Christian Publisher

Based in Northern Ireland, distributing across the world.

www.MauriceWylieMedia.com

NEEDING FURTHER HELP?

WE CAN HELP WITH…

ALL ASPECTS OF BOOK PUBLISHING

E-BOOKS

AUDIOBOOKS

AUTHOR WEBSITES

BOOK & MINISTRY TRAILERS

YOUTUBE VIDEOS

DISTRIBUTION

UNITED KINGDOM, USA, CANADA, ITALY, POLAND, RUSSIA, GERMANY, SOUTH KOREA, AUSTRALIA, INDIA, SPAIN, BRAZIL, AFRICA.

LOW-COST QUALITY BOOK PRINTING DELIVERED TO YOUR ADDRESS IN UNITED KINGDOM & EUROPE

START YOUR OWN PUBLISHING HOUSE.

FRANCHISING IS NOW AVAILABLE.

HAVE YOUR OWN UNIQUE PUBLISHING HOUSE

IN PARTNERSHIP WITH

MAURICE WYLIE MEDIA

WITH YOUR OWN LABEL
WE DO ALL THE WORK, YOU GET ALL THE CREDIT

POTENTIAL IS HUGE
INVESTMENT IS REQUIRED

More information visit
www.MauriceWylieMedia.com

> Good carving presents food; good editing presents impressive storylines.

JOIN

KINGDOM REPS

EXPAND THE GOSPEL AND BE PAID

More information visit
www.MauriceWylieMedia.com

NOTES

NOTES

NOTES

NOTES

NOTES

www.ingramcontent.com/pod-product-compliance
Lightning Source LLC
Chambersburg PA
CBHW071522080526
44588CB00011B/1525